WHAT IS
YOUR
PRACTICE?

Lifelong Growth in the Spirit

Liz Forney and Norvene Vest

Morehouse Publishing
NEW YORK

Morehouse Publishing, 19 East 34th Street, New York, NY 10016

Morehouse Publishing is an imprint of Church Publishing Incorporated.
www.churchpublishing.org

Cover design by Laurie Klein Westhafer
Typeset by Progressive Publishing Services

Library of Congress Cataloging-in-Publication Data

Forney, Liz Barrington.
  What is your practice? : lifelong growth in the spirit/Liz Barrington Forney and Norvene Vest.
    pages cm
  Includes bibliographical references.
  ISBN 978-0-8192-2989-2 (pbk.) – ISBN 978-0-8192-2990-8 (ebook) 1. Spiritual life–Catholic Church. I. Title.
  BX2350.3.F675 2015
  248.4'6–dc23

                                        2015009684

Printed in the United States of America

Contents

Chapter 1

ঙ

The Practice of Lifelong Growth in the Spirit

We are impatient of being on the way
to something unknown, something new.
Yet it is the law of all progress that it is made by
passing through some stages of instability—
and it may take a very long time. . . .
Give our Lord the benefit of believing
that his hand is leading you
and accept the anxiety of feeling yourself
in suspense and incomplete.
—Teilhard de Chardin

Encountering the Mystery

One of my favorite stories tells of a long-ago meeting between some Christian missionaries and a king. After the missionaries speak of their faith and encourage the king to become a Christian, the king asks for advice. His wise one responds, "Your Majesty, when we compare the present life of humans with that time of which we have no knowledge, it seems to me like the swift flight of a lone sparrow through the banqueting-hall where you now sit. . . . Inside there is a comforting fire to warm the room; outside, the wintry storms of snow and rain are raging. This sparrow flies swiftly in through one door of the hall, and out through another. While he is inside, he is safe from the winter

1

storms; but after a few moments of comfort, he vanishes from sight into the darkness whence he came. Similarly, humans appear on earth for a little while, but we know nothing of what went before this life, nor what follows. Therefore if this new teaching can reveal any more certain knowledge, it seems only right that we should follow it."[1]

So eloquently yet simply, the story reveals the human condition: we are creatures bounded by birth and death, conscious that there is something "outside" our finite existence, but uncertain about its nature. Our minds wonder about the world beyond the one we know, while mystics and saints of all ages and faiths have testified to the existence of More Than is apparent.

Even in the decades after the "scientific revolution," Christians affirm the reality of that which is beyond immediate comprehension. Evelyn Underhill, that great student of the mystic life, quite straightforwardly speaks of "the hopelessly irrational character of all great religions: which rest, one and all, on a primary assumption that can never be intellectually demonstrated, much less proved—the assumption that the supra-sensible is somehow important and real, and is intimately connected with human life."[2] Underhill adds that there is "a deep instinct of the human mind that there must be a unity, an orderly plan in the universe," an underlying Vitality, an eternal Becoming.[3] Human union with this reality creates a sense of intense aliveness.

Today the experience of unity with the underlying Vitality of the universe is generally referred to as "spiritual formation." That phrase is a shortcut to experience for which there are really no words. I saw this very clearly some years ago in a conversation with my mother. I was raised as a Christian, attending Sunday school routinely and learning the stories of the Bible. My parents always joined my brother and me in Sunday worship, but later I realized that their primary reason for attending church was a social one—almost everyone in our small town did so and it was a way of establishing social acceptance. There is nothing wrong with such an approach to religion, but it seldom touches the deep Aliveness reaching out to us always. So my mother was puzzled when in later years I became actively involved in spiritual formation work. One day she demanded of me, "So what is this spiritual formation anyway?" I opened my mouth and then closed it, realizing there was no way I could explain to her something she had never experienced (or never acknowledged). She wanted an answer in terms she already understood, and I wanted to invite her into a new way of experiencing the world.

As the two of us authors discussed the possible content of this book, this ambiguity became obvious to us. If pressed, we both might say something like, spiritual formation is a way of life. It is a commitment to find and follow God in every moment of every day. But how can that be put into words, given that God's very self is Mystery? Perhaps the best answer is that spiritual formation is surrendering oneself to wonder.

In our early conversations about components of lifelong spiritual growth, we recalled that any lifelong relationship requires attention, nurture, and mutual love. The practices described here are forms of expression of these components. It is generally the case that God is always going out "ahead" of us, calling us, and creating our desire for deepened relationship. We often discover that some parts of us are actually resisting God's call, perhaps due to fears we have about what might be required of us at this depth. When I confess to my longing for deeper relationship with God, I am also acknowledging that I am not yet complete, but that I myself am at this moment a work in progress, and that is humbling.

How do I love God with all my heart, mind, soul, and strength? The fundamental gift of spiritual practice is belonging to a wide and long stream of people before us who have asked our questions, faced doubts, and left records of practices to help us live what we say we believe. Practices offer a bridge between desire and the inhabiting of a new reality, from "ought" to "is," and from "I should" to "I am." In faithful spiritual practice, we find ourselves upheld, not so much chastised for our sins as rather enabled to respond fully to the call we hear.

All spiritual formation begins with the effort to live a moral and ethical life. As we move more deeply into formation, we find that certain practices are more beneficial to us than others. In Eastern religion, persons known to take spiritual life seriously are often greeted with the question, "What is your Practice?" The meaning in that culture has a specific reference to one of four "yogas." (Yoga is a rich term, derived from the root word "yoke" and thus refers to a discipline whose goal is union with the Holy.) Each yoga is a path intended to be congruent with personal strengths and preference. Reflective persons may take the way of *jnana yoga*, or a path to oneness with the Godhead through knowledge. Persons with a more emotional bent may choose *bhakti yoga*, whose path is toward adoration of God. The third path is *karma yoga*, the path to God through work or action, acknowledging that each outward directed act also internally reacts upon the doer. Finally, *raja yoga* experiments with inner realities to observe the effects of various practices upon one's spiritual condition.[4]

Christian practice does not make this distinction between specialized paths, rather offering a variety of possibilities, all of which are aimed at living a life attuned to the Gospel. Each individual is encouraged to explore many practices, gradually discovering those most conducive to deepened relationship with God.

Standing in Relation: God's "Kindom"

The core of Christian spiritual life is the conviction that *relationship with Mystery* is not only possible but essential for a full human life. Jesus of Nazareth teaches his disciples to call the Mystery Abba, father. We need not literalize his words to envision an old man in the sky, but clearly Jesus believed that his contact with the Mystery was intimate and personal, and that everyone is invited to such a relationship. He modeled the quality of personal intimacy every time he invited someone to "come and see," gathered a group of friends in ministry, and sat at table with all manner of people.[5]

> **Pause to reflect:** *Take a moment to ponder your personal sense of how you are being invited to live in relationship with God. You might write for a few moments about the longing and hopes you feel as you begin reading this book.*

Jesus announces his ministry with the words, "The Kingdom of God is at hand" (Matt. 4:17, Mk. 1:15, Lk. 10:9). The meaning of these words further unfolds the nature of the invitation to relationship. The phrase "at hand" is one that theologians have pondered deeply, but it clearly means that in some sense the kingdom is already present, that a new era has arrived marked by the constant operation of divine power. It has something to do with Jesus, and it is not fully present as yet, but it is *available*, not just to Jesus but to everyone.

"Kingdom" is a word not used much in contemporary Western secular settings, so it is a little more difficult to understand. Again theologians have studied its meaning, and sometimes it seems to refer to time (the dramatic moment of arrival), and sometimes to space (the "realm" God rules). The Greek term is *basileia*, which can be interpreted as commonweal. Ada Maria Isasi-Diaz prefers the contemporary term "*kindom*," suggesting an inclusive community of relationships.[6] Thus Jesus is affirming a present realm or community in which the holy can be experienced every day by every person.

The realm is now at hand, and it calls for "repentance." Fundamentally, repentance means a change of direction, a turning around. Although response to Jesus's announcement is often interpreted as referring to a single moment of radical insight, after which a person repents of "sinfulness" and vows to live a new life, the ideas above suggest a more nuanced response. The overall theme of this book is a human response to Jesus's call to live in God's *baseleia* is not a one-time thing. There may indeed be a moment (or more than one) when we feel suddenly washed through with blessing and hope, and desire to make a commitment to a different kind of life. But like New Year's resolutions, the initial commitment is only the beginning. Response to God's invitation is in fact a lifelong task, involving various practices over time. Perhaps Jesus's disciples initially understood his call to follow him as a big commitment, but one that only asked of them their initial response. Nevertheless, they passed through many stages of confusion and doubt, found themselves sorely distressed and greatly tried, and were often disappointed in themselves (and sometimes even in Jesus). If we believe that the only thing necessary to live a full spiritual life is an initial commitment, we are likely to find ourselves similarly restless or simply bored.

Practicing Relationship with Mystery

Fundamentally, lifelong spiritual practice, or spiritual formation, refers to the means by which we learn to experience our relationship with Mystery over a long period. It may seem curious or puzzling to consider nurturing a relationship with the One who is and will always be much of a mystery to us. It may help to think about our own spiritual formation in the image of a seed unfolding.

First, there exists the seed itself, with its unique potential. We may imagine this seed is the soul of each one of us, personally called forth from God with the words "I love you." Josef Pieper observes that in the act of creation, God says to each and all: "I will you to be; it is good, 'very good' (Gen. 1:31) that you exist."[7]

Gradually the seed unfolds. Planted and sprouting, it must grow. But it grows better if tended. Certainly this involves help outside ourselves, helpless as we are in the beginning, but it also involves our willingness, even our eagerness to become. Thus we know that what happens in the unfolding is a work of co-creation: God is at work in us, and we are cooperating with God.

Formation is the interaction between potential and nurturance. God is involved in both aspects; we are largely involved in the latter, insuring that nutrients are provided by good soil, water, sun, fertilizer as necessary. In a human life, this includes the classic spiritual practices of prayer and worship, study, work and community. Through worship and study we learn about taking on the mind of Christ and becoming the body of Christ. Through work and community we learn that every moment of the day provides an opportunity to practice our desire and intent. Practices build habits and enlarge our hearts, helping us strengthen our awareness of God as companion in our dailyness, and bringing us a subtle ever-present depth of joy.

It is, of course, much easier to say this than to do it. The constancy of practice can seem a burden. The hiddenness of results can be discouraging. And life provides so many opportunities to "go to seed"—times when it feels our vitality is diminished by involuntary losses of cherished ideas or beloved persons. Yet here too Christ is with us: the cross and resurrection teach us that dying is not the end, but rather the doorway to new life.

All this is vastly different from the cultural notions that surround us. This process of spiritual formation is not primarily managed, analytical-objective, individual, or even what we might call "successful." Yet for those desiring a strong and flexible spiritual life and an ongoing maturity in relationship with God, practice is invaluable. What we desire and need is already near us, supporting and strengthening our faith, hope, and love.

Lifelong spiritual growth involves several key points:

- Conviction that as human beings, God's spirit engages us in an ongoing relationship without which life would be less than full and empty of abundance;
- Willingness to undertake a guided discipline for integration of self, pulling pieces and parts into a harmonizing whole in a way that gives meaning and purpose in life;
- Affirmation that we are (still) formable and can take part in our own formation;
- Finally, for Christians, the central dimension of spirituality is knowing and being known by, loving and being strengthened by, Jesus Christ.

The Commandment to Love Ourselves

"The first is, . . . you shall love your God with all your heart, your soul, your mind and strength. The second is you shall love your neighbor as yourself." (Mark 12:29-30, modified)

We have heard much about these words of Jesus and we take them to heart, especially when it comes to the God part and the neighbor part. But if we take seriously the other two aspects, why do we forget the third: loving ourselves? More importantly, why might God care that we love ourselves?

Self-love is neither arrogance nor selfishness. It is taking seriously the potential God places in us to become who we most truly are. God loves each of us into being specifically—a uniqueness, an originality that matters. Each of us is meant to become the whole person we carry as seed within us. Each carries a potential meant for full development, not the same as everyone else, but embodying our own specific vocation or call from God to be. God's call is issued in love, and our lives are sustained by love in continuous unfolding to a particular some-thing which only we are.

When we are truly living to our potential, we feel a quality of personal wholeness inside. Scripture is full of words that describe the abundance Jesus brings. The baskets of food collected *after* feeding the five thousand are *overflowing* (Mark 6:42-3). After Jesus tells a weary crew to down their nets *again*, the fish caught are so heavy that the nets might break (Luke 5:1-6). The presence of God involves not only the absence of anxiety, but also the reality of something generous and full of gladness, as natural as can be.

To love ourselves is to give ourselves permission to live in this state of abundant, full wholeness. It is already here. God has claimed that state, intends it for each one of us, and thus is at work within us helping to bring it about. God loves us unconditionally; who are we to withhold love from ourselves?

Learning to love ourselves and experience wholeness is not easy. It may indeed be one of the most difficult practices of the spiritual life. We have many old memories, habits of protection, learned defenses that hold God away. Experiencing God's presence as loving-kindness is not so much a matter of periodic saving eruptions in our lives, as rather the ongoing formative blessing that is somewhat harder to notice, because so near to us. It will not happen at once, and it will not prevent "bad things happening." But it will give us the peace, serenity, and passion to address what we must, and leave the rest to God. When we encounter fear, we can let it become an ally in the certainty that we have encountered *something that can be transformed* by God's grace.

It requires work and patience to discover the inner desire that is God's flight encircling us. Yet that is indeed what we are called to do.

In short, lifelong spirituality is openness to relationship, first with God, then with self and other. This openness results in heightened or expanded consciousness and behavior, and is shaped by one's particular tradition. Lifelong spirituality, or formative spirituality, involves awareness that everything we do and/or that is done to us *shapes* or *forms* us in some way. Some habits and influences can be deformative. The focus of spiritual formation is on attending to God's desires for us and in us and allowing our lives to be shaped by those desires. Since God is always somewhat hidden, spiritual formation requires regular habits and practice that help us become more attentive to the divine presence within our daily lives. The practices in this book are intended to help us do so.

Potential Impediments

At best, a lifelong spiritual practice can be difficult as well as rewarding. It may help to understand why practice is so essential in the present time if we turn to a bit of recent religious history in the United States. Sociologist Robert Wuthnow's book *After Heaven*[8] traces the changes in American spiritual life and the way we have understood the sacred in the last half of the twentieth century. He describes a movement from a spirituality of dwelling (centered in a stable and sacred place) to a spirituality of seeking (where one must constantly renegotiate the meaning of transient glimpses of the sacred). In-depth interviews of some two hundred people suggest that faith is no longer something people inherit but something for which they strive, seeking connections with various organizations and disciplines while yet feeling marginal to any particular group or place.[9] As the common web of assumptions supporting the older pattern began to fray in the '70s and '80s, religious practice became that of *search*. Search is something of an eclectic matter, perhaps finding community in Sunday services, but also seeking out such things as a yoga class, a Buddhist meditation retreat, and so forth. The movement away from the older practice of dwelling corresponds to a cultural shift involving commuting or frequent moves connected with employment and the consequent disconnection from family and traditional home places—a radical expansion of the world in terms of information flows, and an increasing emphasis on consumption and entertainment. This movement is also linked to the shift from an orderly, systematic understanding of life to a bewildering variety of worldviews and philosophies of life on offer in our midst. Wuthnow suggests that "the United States is moving into an era of what might be termed a 'thin consensus' in which relatively few values are held in common."[10]

Reflecting on these two approaches to spirituality, Wuthnow finds each one incomplete: dwelling because of its relatively rigid emphasis on a distinction between the sacred and the profane, and seeking because of its inevitable focus on individual gratification. He suggests that to retrieve balance in this new century, "the ancient wisdom that emphasizes the idea of *spiritual practices* needs to be rediscovered."[11]

We can even think of Jesus himself teaching a practice-oriented spirituality, though he blends it with aspects of what we have called dwelling, involving setting aside a space in which to meditate, pray, and worship. Yet for him, such spaces are changeable, depending on circumstances, and the point of withdrawal is not merely to feel secure in a sacred space but to grow increasingly aware of the mysterious and transcendent aspects of the One who guides him. His practice was sometimes undertaken alone, but was often undertaken in the company of others. Practice apparently involves self-reflection and challenge, includes moral dimensions, and in the experience of connection to the Divine Center, offers cautious hope for each day. Jesus's practice-oriented spirituality models a rigorous life devoted to deepening his relationship with Abba.

The tradition of spiritual practice was not lost after Jesus's death. Paul's letters reveal his commitment to regular spiritual practice as foundational to his ministry, as do other New Testament books. Christian leaders throughout the centuries such as Benedict of Nursia, Calvin, Luther, Teresa of Avila, Ignatius of Loyola and others also testify to wisdom-guided spiritual practice, not just in the beginning of their lives and ministry, but throughout it. All these leaders left books or records, fortunately translated into English, and they can be our friends and guides even now.

Unfortunately, at some point in Christian history, the notion seemed to rise that such spiritual practices were meant only for would-be saints, or for vowed religious and ordained persons. The practices themselves continued to be kept alive, but for a very small group of people, and often were more focused on identification with the charism of the particular office or community rather than on ongoing relationship with the Mystery.

Also, the contemporary emphasis on the scientifically demonstrable in the West has gradually led our institutions, including our religious

institutions, away from ongoing conversations about values and meaning which rest in experiences of God. On the whole, western Christians
are skeptical of mystical affirmations, preferring to "lay ahold" of real
and practical things. So we who hope to live a full and vibrant religious
life are left with many questions. How do I talk with God? How do I
experience God, not only in prayer, but as a vital and living presence
in my life? Are such experiences "real"? If so, how do I love God with
all my heart, mind, soul, and strength? We may, indeed, desire these
things, but we hardly know how or where to begin.

A Return to Practice

This book is intended to answer some of these questions by offering
a variety of Christian practices, some traditional and some modified
in contemporary language to speak to the holiness of daily life when
lived in the awareness of God's presence. The practices offered in these
pages help build a bridge between desire and the inhabiting of a new
reality of lifelong growth in the Spirit, of intentional and fruitful spiritual formation. How is growth in the Spirit different from regular
church attendance and concern for the poor? Our terms *center specifically on the relationship with God.* Of course, spiritual formation does not
exclude attending church nor caring for the poor, but those activities
are seen as actions growing from relationship with God. The reality
of spiritual formation does not depend on how we *think* about God
(because God is greater than anything we can think), as long as we
have *a desire to be in relationship with God* and believe that God desires to
be in relationship with us.

The Mystery that is God chooses to reach out to each one of us and
something within the nature of the human being responds. Paschal
speaks of a "God-shaped vacuum" within the human, a part of our
essence that is incomplete unless in relationship with the Divine Being.
The foundations of such a relationship can be thought of as emerging
not primarily in a setting governed by sin and repentance, but rather
by call and response. God is always reaching out (calling) and our
yearning for the More is response to that originating call. God's loving
movement toward creation forms the basis for spiritual formation.

The unexpected joy of this process is that what God calls to us
matches the shape of our own deep wholeness. A sense of personal
wholeness is not the same thing as personal gratification, of course.
The ongoing relationship with God teaches us to reach more deeply

into our best selves, and to discover anew how to be the persons we most hope to be, even in circumstances not of our choice. As we progress in our spiritual growth toward and with God, we discover a personal sense of rightness and completeness that is precisely what we would have chosen, could we have known ahead of time what was possible for us. But usually we must begin the journey without knowing the fullness of what lies ahead, because in the beginning our hearts are not large enough for that knowing. Much of what happens in lifelong spiritual growth happens outside our immediate awareness, because after all, it is God's work within us, not a matter of what our own executive will can accomplish. We have a choice: we can consent to and cooperate with this great work or not. Indeed, our practice is an essential element of the process, but our ego is not the "boss." We may often *feel* that nothing at all is going on, but usually we can look back and see how profoundly we are changing for our own good and the good of others. Underneath all practice is humility, the willingness to proceed *without knowing*.

The unknowingness, the sense of things happening without our control, is put into formal language in the classic definition of spiritual theology as including two parts, one called ascetical and one called mystical. Ascetical refers to efforts on the human side to reach toward God, to eliminate those habits or patterns that move us away from the holy, and to learn to see with God's eyes. Mystical refers, in the words of a twelfth century monk, to the fact that God "does not wait until the longing soul has said all its say, but breaks in upon the middle of its prayer, runs to meet it in all haste, . . . and restores the weary soul, slakes its thirst, feeds its hunger, . . . and gives it new life in a wonderful way."[12] God comes to us even before we know what we long for. Although this book emphasizes practice—the ascetical side—it does so with full awareness that the "effectiveness" of our practice depends utterly on God's doing within us. However hard or wearisome or even glorious our practice seems to us, it is ultimately God's work happening in our unknowing. I have often taken heart from Abbot John Chapman's assurance that however dry, weak, or unsatisfactory our practice seems, if we are doing our best the result is just exactly what God wants us to have here and now.[13] How we *feel* about our practice is far less important than that the core of our soul is sticking to God.

Practice is seldom easy, but it does offer a way to live what we say we believe. It involves a movement from head knowledge (mainly study and analysis) to heart knowledge (mainly embracing, the organ capable of reaching into God's being in God's self and in creation). Practice in spirituality is not dissimilar from practice in piano or tennis: we are not capable of instant results, and it is effortful, but sustained over time, it begins to seem more "natural" and more rewarding. The analogy fails if pushed too far, however, because pianos and tennis courts are not persons, and we are seeking a relationship—not just any relationship, but one with a Mysterious Other whose ways are always more than we can comprehend. As anyone who has ever tried to condense a genuine relationship into "quality time" knows, speed inhibits relationality.

It is ironic that we tend both to desire and to resist God's in-breaking in our lives, for fear that we will lose our independence, our freedom. It helps to recognize that resistance in ourselves, so we can push through it when it arises. In the long run, the disciplines of practice offer greater freedom than anything we might imagine will have to be relinquished in faithful practice. In the following chapters, we will discuss not only what each practice is and how to make it workable for yourself, but also some barriers you might encounter as you proceed. It is not a shame to encounter discouraging moments; the only shame is to try to be God rather than to love God.

Using this Book with a Small Group

Community is essential in the spiritual life. We naturally need the encouragement and shared experience of others who are seeking intimacy with God. Jesus himself chose twelve friends with whom to share the journey and face the challenges of following God. While this resource is written for individual use, it can also be adapted for use in a small group.

One of the most important aspects of using this book with others will be the development of intimacy and trust. You might invite others whom you know well to do a book study together, or reach out into the community for other seekers to join you on this adventure. The first meeting should be about getting to know one another and cultivating hopes and expectations for your time together.

Questions for the group to ponder include:

- Who will facilitate each meeting?
- What is the best time frame for your gathering?
- Would you like it to include some social time, or be more contemplative?

It can help the process to begin with the creation of a covenant for the group that helps each person feel safe and honored. A covenant is really just an agreement about what is hoped for from members in the way of things like participation, commenting on what one another shares, and confidentiality. Participants might begin by sharing past successful experiences of small groups and what is most important for each member in the way of creating a sense of security and community. For many people it is important that members of the group commit to being present each time the group gathers and not just popping in when it is convenient. It is often helpful to ask that members refrain from offering advice or commentary on what another shares, but simply listen and affirm what each member offers. It is also important to be aware of differences in temperaments. Extroverts can be encouraged to hold onto their thoughts and insights for just a bit longer than they normally would, while introverts might be encouraged to speak up.

Each chapter includes questions with an invitation to pause and reflect. These can be used to facilitate group sharing and insights. They are just a beginning point for your group to process the ideas offered in the chapters. At the end of each chapter you will find sample exercises. Participants might be encouraged to choose a practice that feels inviting or challenging to them and to practice it in the intervening time between group meetings.

After the initial meeting in which folks get to know one another, share hopes, and create a covenant, a sample group gathering outline might look like this:

- Time in centering silence inviting God to direct and be present with the group.
- Group gathering with brief check in about highlights in each person's life.
- Review the chapter contents and main ideas discussing the pauses to reflect.
- Share questions and comments about the chapter.
- Look over the exercises and each person choose a practice.
- The following meeting, check in time might include reflections on how the practice went. Where did you notice God? How were you challenged or encouraged in this practice? How might you amend this practice going forward?

This is not a "how to" book. We do not offer "six steps to spiritual success!" because we do not believe growth in the spirit lends itself to formulas. Instead we offer reflections and specifics on practices found both in Christian spiritual tradition and the best of modern psychology as leading toward spiritual maturity and psychological wholeness.

We are both Protestant Christians, Liz an ordained Presbyterian pastor and Norvene a lay Episcopalian and oblate of St. Benedict. Liz has teenage children and Norvene has great-grandchildren by marriage. We both are well-married, challenged often by our spouses, and supported always. We are white, educated, and moderately well-off, and we acknowledge that means we have certain blind spots in our understandings. We ask that you not imagine that either of us are "experts." It is perhaps presumptuous to write a book such as this, but we write as much from our own inadequacies as from our strengths. Please use this book for reflection in light of your own experiences of God, and follow the Spirit as you find yourself called. We'll be praying for you, even as we ask you to pray for us.

We offer this book as what might be thought of as a reference book about key tools in lifelong spiritual growth. As we both are Christians, our desire is to present the rich array of tools available from the Christian tradition, some of which seem to have been hidden away in more recent times. However, we also hope that persons who identify with other spiritual traditions may find some of these tools helpful. While as a reader you may wish at first to read straight through the book, we encourage you to return to various sections to work primarily with each one at different times. We think of this as a "reference book," because our experience is that for persons of varying temperaments, or for a single person throughout a lifetime, differing practices may be of value at different times. *May you be blessed.*

SAMPLE EXERCISES

1. Take some time to check in with yourself and reflect on where you are at present in your relationship with God. You might begin by finishing the following sentence, "God and I are_____." After you finish your reflections about where you are at present you might take some time to map out where you and God have been. Use the following questions as writing prompts:
   - Was there a time when you felt especially close to God? What was that like? If you have not had a time like that, do you desire a close relationship? What do you imagine it would be like?

- Can you remember your childhood image of God? How has it changed over the years?
- Has God mostly been an idea, a set of shoulds, oughts, and rules, or a real and loving presence for you?
- As you reflect on where you and God have been, do you have a glimpse of where you are being invited to go in your relationship with God?

2. Take some time to sit in silence and ponder the possibility and assertion that God is reaching for you and seeking a sincere and affectionate relationship with you. Hold in your heart and mind the truth that God is moving towards you with the intention of nourishing, encouraging, and directing your life. Just let that idea be in you and move in you. Notice the thoughts and feelings that arise as you hold this idea. When you are ready, compose a prayer of consent to God as you begin this journey.

FOR FURTHER READING

Borg, Marcus J. *The Heart of Christianity: Rediscovering a Life of Faith.* San Francisco: HarperCollins, 2003.

Johnson, Jan. *Abundant Simplicity: Discovering the Unhurried Rhythms of Grace.* Downers Grove, IL: IVP Books, 2011.

Mulholland, M. Robert Jr. *Invitation to a Journey: A Road Map for Spiritual Formation.* Downers Grove, IL: Intervarsity Press, 1993.

Muller, Wayne. *Sabbath: Finding Rest, Renewal, and Delight in Our Busy Lives.* New York: Bantam Books, 1999.

Nolan, Albert. *Jesus Today: A Spirituality of Radical Freedom.* Maryknoll, NY: Orbis Books, 2006.

Robinson, David. *Ancient Paths: Discover Christian Formation the Benedictine Way.* Brewster, MA: Paraclete Press, 2010.

Rohlheiser, Ronald. *The Holy Longing: The Search for a Christian Spirituality.* New York: Doubleday, 1999.

Vanier, Jean. *Becoming Human.* New York: Paulist Press, 1998.

Chapter 2

అ

Gratitude, Attention, and Awareness: The Practice of Presence

Gratitude bestows reverence,
allowing us to encounter everyday epiphanies,
those transcendent moments of awe
that change forever how we experience life and the world.
Sarah Ban Breathnach

"O, give thanks to the Lord, for God's steadfast love endures forever." These words echo over and over again in an ecstatic refrain in both Psalm 118 and 136. They are a declaration, a command, a statement of faith, and a hymn of praise all woven together. They give voice to a shout of joy announcing that something astonishing and unexpectedly delightful has happened. As we join in this prayer our knees are buckling, our hands are raised overhead, and tears tug at the edge of our eyes. Perhaps a child is born, or the raw beauty of life has finally shimmered through the dull dust of repetitive days. The lab tests have come back negative for cancer, or the loved one has returned home unharmed. Somehow these words testify to a God who showed up, a love that broke through, and a Spirit that stirred, making gratitude the only possible response. These are the days when words of thanks come readily and easily, when "God's in heaven and all's right with the world."[1]

Give Thanks in All Things?

But what about those days that are not so filled with joy? What about the days when it is all we can do to get up and face the world one more day? How do we honor the psalmist's invitation and God's command to give thanks when all our words stick like dry toast in the back of our throat? There are many days when the command or invitation to give thanks can feel like the nudge from our parents to thank Aunt Edna for the lovely (hideous) gift sweater. The sweater is simply unwearable and saying "thank you" feels like a huge lie. If we were honest about it, we would return the gift. Sadly, that feeling is a rather common part of our journey through life, and there is no return policy for days that fall far short of our hopes and expectations.

Somehow, and not surprisingly, it is actually on those difficult days and in those heavy seasons that the disciplined practice of gratitude is most essential, most powerful, and most life giving. To develop a posture of gratitude when we feel we are drowning is to cultivate confidence in the God who surrounds us despite what can sometimes seem to be significant evidence to the contrary. As we practice gratitude in all situations we find that our way of viewing and experiencing the world is changed. The effort that it sometimes takes to find something worthy of praise begins to open our eyes to the gifts that surround us daily. It takes time and a measure of commitment to train our eyes and hearts to see the holy, the beautiful, and the blessed in what sometimes feels like a dim and broken world. Not only does this practice alter our outward vision and our ability to see God's hand at work in the world, but as we continue on this pathway, this new way of seeing the world leads us to a new way of being in the world as our interior landscape expands with joy, humility, and praise.

The healing and transforming power of the practice of gratitude became piercingly real for a small group of dear friends during our sophomore year in college. Like many other students—during what is so aptly named the sophomore slump—one of us descended into a dark season. Unlike others she was not able to shake it off with a jog, or an art class, or a pair of snappy new shoes. Eating and sleeping were problematic for her. She would show up at meals and barely eat anything. All of us who were close friends with her were very worried for her. We invited her to parties and to go shopping, but she said that things that had been joyful and fun were simply flat and too effortful. She would be in class and we could see the heaviness just hanging on her.

We urged her to go to the counseling center on campus. Thankfully she found a great person there who listened deeply and cared well for her. After a few weeks we began to notice a small shift.

When we asked her what changed, she said that, among other things, the therapist had given her an exercise that she was to do daily, without fail, to help restore balance to an overwhelmingly bitter and burdened interior narrative. Each night before going to bed she had to make a list of ten things that were okay. If she got out of bed in the morning, it counted. Having a cup of tea could be counted. Noticing a bird could go on the list. She was not to rest until she had listed ten things that were not the pain and misery that seemed to surround every movement. It actually became a blessing for all of us in that small circle. As we would notice good things—a sunset, the taste of ice cream, how grass smells when it is first cut—we would say to one another, "that should go on the list." All of us began to find our outlooks improved by being on the lookout for the goodness in life.

While my friend's experience was one of a general outlook of gratitude that brought a measure of healing, Luke's gospel tells another story of the healing power of gratitude. In this story, the way a sense of gratitude leads one into relationship with Jesus is transformational. According to the passage, as Jesus was traveling between Samaria and Galilee he encountered a small community of lepers who cried out to him for mercy. He responded with compassion and told them to go and show themselves to the priests. This wasn't a brush off, but the formal way by which their healing could be verified and they would be reinstated back into the community. All ten dashed off toward the temple, but as they were going one of them was moved on some deeper level. His recognition of the gift, his heartfelt gratitude, made him turn back to Jesus where he fell on his knees and praised God for the miracle that had occurred. Jesus looks for the other nine, seemingly a bit sad that they thought so little of his gift. What happened next is an unexpected twist. Jesus told the man, "Get up and go on your way; your faith has made you well" (Luke 17:11-19). Far from a repeat of his earlier miracle, Jesus was doing something new in this encounter grounded in gratitude. A closer look at the text tells us that Jesus's first word to the lepers made them all *clean*, but this encounter of praise and relationship with Christ made the one who returned to give thanks truly *whole*. It is as if the single leper, by grace of his awareness of both the gift and the giver was given a second blessing. He was able to pause and put aside, at least for a moment, all the fantasies he had cultivated in his suffering on the edge of community about how he would run home and rejoin his family and friends. For just a moment, he was aware that something truly holy was happening and he wanted to fully take it in and participate in praise. That pause of awareness is at the heart of the practice of gratitude.

Moving with a sense of presence and attention through each day returns us again and again into the realm of the divine. What is required is the discipline not to get caught up in the tiny dust storms and flurry of fretting that are so constant and familiar in much of modern life. A spiritually mature life requires that we repeatedly turn from distractions and small mindedness and instead cultivate the willingness to set our eyes and hearts on the goodness that God makes available to us at every turn.

A Balanced Outlook

Wisdom and guidance for this comes to us in the passage from Philippians: "Finally, beloved, whatever is true, whatever is honorable, whatever is just, whatever is pure, whatever is pleasing, whatever is commendable, if there is any excellence and if there is anything worthy of praise, think about these things" (Phillipians 4:8). It is a mystery for the ages and an undeniable truth that, for the most part, we are drawn toward the darkness and we allow ourselves to focus on what is not right, what is displeasing, and those things we want to oppose. Fear muddies our outlook and distorts our vision. The evening news and most headlines are full of a sense of impending doom and chaos. If we are not to be swallowed in the swamp of despair, we have to train our hearts and eyes to attend to the goodness that surrounds us, and to return again and again to God with thanksgiving.

A Matter of Perspective

Both the story of the healing of the lepers and the letter to the Philippians invite us to consider the way in which the exact same situation can be experienced and viewed from a number of different perspectives. We can see life through the tight lens of cynicism, critique, and scarcity, or through the spacious window of abundance and appreciation. It is also possible, as writers in the contemplative tradition suggest, to view and respond to life in a posture blended somewhere in between. Always there will be aspects of reality to grieve over, and still others to praise. The gift is that we get to choose how we want to view and experience this journey.

This past Easter as I helped with refreshments between the worship services I witnessed just such a paradox. Members of the congregation were invited to bring a treat to share with one another as they visited, and a gorgeous table of muffins, cookies, fruit, cheese, and crackers was laid out for all to enjoy. One member passed through the kitchen and rejoiced, "Look at that beautiful abundance of goodies." One breath later, another member came in and asked with alarm, "Have you been in the sanctuary? It's packed, and this will all be gone in minutes." Both statements were true, but one conveyed an energy and spirit of appreciation, which uplifted all of us in the kitchen. The other almost knocked the wind right out of our sails. Our lives unfold by the narrative we tell ourselves. What we look for we will see, be it beauty or brokenness, fullness or fragments. The way in which we choose to view all of life will alter our experience of it. As we strengthen the spiritual muscles of appreciation and as we cultivate interior awareness of both our grasping and repulsions, we grow in our ability to loosen the poisonous grip of the illusion of scarcity.

Have you ever noticed that there are only a very few mental postures we usually take when we encounter anything? In a matter of seconds we seem to make a snap evaluation of the person, object, or situation before us. It is only a slight oversimplification to say that either we see beauty and want to somehow possess it, or we see a threat and we want to avoid it. There is a third way: the way of simple presence. This posture of simple presence can help us navigate the stormy waters of emotions and judgments and can aid us in our desire to dwell in gratitude. What is meant by simple presence is cultivation of the ability to simply be with a person or in a situation as it presents itself. In this posture of presence, we are invited to resist judgment and evaluation. As we deepen our connection to the Holy and expand our awareness of the unity and fullness in all creation, we are freed to have something of a detached perspective that allows us to see the reflection of God in all things and that moves us to praise and deeper love.

In *Living Simply through the Day*,[2] Tilden Edwards, the founder of the Shalem Institute and its Senior Fellow, offers us a rich resource for expanding our capacity for appreciation of God and all of life by inviting us to fully indwell the presence of God throughout our day. The book is also a gift for those looking to cultivate a posture of loving presence in the world and working to be freed from the tangles of attachment, evaluation, and unnecessary striving. From the moment we wake, to the way in which we consume our food, Edwards calls us again and again to simple appreciation and presence with God. Before we leave the comfort of the bed, we might consider not turning on the radio, or checking our smart phone for email and the day's to do list, but rather directing our attention to the Holy One who has seen us through the night and given us the gift of another day. As we begin to enter the day we are invited to gently engage our bodies by stretching and with mindfulness open our hearts and minds to the inter-connectedness of all things. Where we focus our attention will greatly influence the flow of our days and the depth of our appreciation. We are free to focus on the landslide of undone tasks and unmet desires, or we can savor God's provision and respond in thanksgiving in each encounter of the day.

This type of mindful living requires practice involving the unlearning of many of the ways that we have been taught to engage the world. Becoming aware of the internal pushes and pulls we face each day is the place to begin. Once we are aware of the ways in which we strive for approval or actively work to avoid pain and challenge, then we are empowered to make a new choice. As we invite God into all those interactions, we make ourselves available for God's healing and transformation.

Detractors to Gratitude

Though there are many detractors to the grace of gratitude, there are two in particular that we will explore here: comparison and expectations.

Among the many distractors from our sense of gratitude, few are as powerful as the poison of comparison. In this era of social media where everyone is publishing the grandness of their own lives, snapping and sharing photos of their amazing vacations or the achievements of their children, it can be nearly impossible to avoid comparing and finding one's life seemingly lacking. Studies at both the University of Michigan and the University of Gothenburg, Sweden found that the more time one spent on Facebook, the lower one's self-esteem and wellbeing.[3] Instead of appreciating the goodness and gifts we have been given, we are in danger of becoming a people who believe that someone else always has it better than we do. The dumpster of disappointment is not far from the field of comparing. The truth is there will be parties we are not invited to, opportunities that are not afforded to us, and beautiful places we will never see, but that reality should not keep us from noticing and rejoicing in what we have been given.

At Christmas a few years back our kids were delighted with the simple gifts, books, and experiences they had received. We had enjoyed some wonderful family time and even had a trip to Colorado to visit extended family. All was well until the first day back to school after vacation. The obligatory recitation of Christmas gifts was held on the bus, and it seemed that other kids had far more to brag about. What followed was a very painful and powerful conversation. We got to reflect on how happy we had been just that morning and how the pain only came in the comparison. The grass on our side of the fence is plenty green, and surely sufficient, but so often it sure does look better on the other side.

Pause to reflect:
- In what ways do you compare yourself and your life with others?
- How does this comparison with others encourage or discourage your spirit?
- How does comparison affect your relationship with others?
- Is there a way you might move toward a posture of appreciation and gratitude without comparison?

It sometimes seems that if we aren't tripping over comparison with others, we are stubbing our toes on the rocks of expectation and entitlement. For most of us living in North America we take many of our conveniences for granted and assume they are there for our pleasure. If we turn on the tap and the water does not come out clean and at the desired temperature we can get pretty upset. We expect the grocery stores to be stocked with options and delicacies, and when we flip a switch the lights and the computer should come on. These are basic daily events that in other parts of the world would be wonders and cause for joy.

Sometimes we need an experience of loss or dislocation to open us again to gratitude. The soft bed feels best after sleeping on the hard ground. The hot food tastes fabulous when we have missed a meal or two. Each day becomes priceless and sacred when we are unsure of the number of days we have left. When we are blessed enough to be taken out of our sense of entitlement and expectation, we can be opened to a new kind of joy and appreciation for unexpected gifts. The spiritual journey is one of emptying and filling again like ocean waves going out and coming in. We release and surrender, and allow God to fill us anew.

Over the years my husband and I have moved a number of times as the Spirit has called us to new ministries. Each time I grieve leaving the people and community with which I have become familiar and with whom I have shared precious memories. I also grieve leaving the flower gardens I had spent countless hours cultivating. In our most recent move I had the delightful experience during the first spring in our new house of walking through the yard with utter delight as each blossoming surprise unfolded. I had not planted anything. I did not even know what some of the tree species were, since we had arrived in the fall and the leaves were gone and many of the flowerbeds faded. Daffodils came up and dogwoods cascaded around us, and I knew I could take credit for none of it. The hedge that I thought was some odd kind of boxwood was actually a gardenia bush and the blossoms were simply stunning! We watched as gift after gift unfolded and we delighted in each new discovery. I enjoyed that spring more than any other I can remember because I experienced it as pure gift. By grace I had been freed from expectations or pride and was instead filled with gratitude for all that appeared.

Perhaps this is a window into the power of what Paul writes in Ephesians 2: 4-9:

> "But God, who is rich in mercy, out of the great love with which he loved us even when we were dead through our trespasses, made us alive together with Christ—by grace you have been saved—and raised us up with him and seated us with him in the heavenly places in Christ Jesus, so that in the ages to come he might show the immeasurable riches of his grace in kindness toward us in Christ Jesus. *For by grace you have been saved through faith, and this is not your own doing; it is the gift of God—not the result of works, so that no one may boast."*

Gratitude emerges from the simple and profound realization that we didn't create this world and its beauty. Open-hearted appreciation unfolds as we deepen our awareness to the loving presence of God that is available and surrounds us always. This gracious awareness expands as we practice turning away from comparison, expectation, and grasping and move towards simple presence. This movement will invite a new practice of stillness and contemplation.

Gratitude and Inner Stillness

All of us are surrounded by competing voices, stories, and chatter—both internal and external. In contrast to that noise and chaos, deep within each of us, under the tumult and crashing waves there is a pool of stillness, wisdom, and grace. All of the wisdom traditions speak of the practice of engaging the holiness of stillness and interior silence. For some it is called meditation, and others call it contemplative or centering prayer. In the Christian tradition as early as the sixth century, Gregory the Great spoke of the practice of contemplation as the "knowledge of God that is impregnated with love."[4] In all cases, what is being invoked is a centered presence from which to engage the world. In many ways, the practice of the presence of God is one way in which we can begin to enact our longing and Jesus's calling to "love the Lord your God with all your heart, mind, soul, and strength" (Deuteronomy 6:5). As we begin to practice first connecting to and then living from this center of stillness, we find that we have an anchor, a home, an inner sacred space that grounds us and allows us to move out into the world in freedom and joy.

We are given a similar image of a home base from which to move out into the world in Robert W. Russell's, *To Catch an Angel; Adventures in a World I Cannot See.*[5] In it he tells stories of his life and the challenges and adventures he encountered living without sight. As a child, he tells us, birds seemed like angels to him. One of the most evocative passages in the book is his story of wanting to be able to row his boat out on a river. He knows such a dream is dangerous and purely wild folly. He has no doubt that should he attempt such a thing he will be lost to the current and never find his way home again. Finally, he comes upon a brilliant solution. He installs a bell on the end of the dock to chime at regular intervals. He launches his boat cautiously into the current of the river and rows as far out as he can while still able to hear the sound of the bell. When the sound of his bell becomes too faint he knows it is time to row for home. Our practice of contemplative prayer, of being quiet daily with dedicated attention before God, can serve for us as such a sounding bell. To begin though, we will need to create the center of quiet within.

It is entirely possible that you may have actually practiced contemplative prayer without even knowing it. The first step of this spiritual discipline is notice your breathing; the simple in and out flow of breath. Next, just begin to pay attention to your body, where you are holding tension, where there might be a hint of pain. As you become quieter, you might realize that this still presence is vaguely familiar. Anyone who has ever nursed a newborn, or rocked a baby to sleep knows the stillness of this sacred gaze. Anyone who has ever lain on their back in a field and gazed up in to the night sky knows this loss of self into a greater whole. If you have spent even an hour simply watching the flames in the fireplace, allowing the warmth to melt you and quiet your racing mind, you are quite close to this practice.

Father Thomas Keating, one of the most well regarded authors on the practice of contemplative prayer, helps us fine-tune the essence of this practice when he reminds us that contemplative prayer is not about relaxation, but rather about relationship. What we are seeking in contemplative prayer is a deepening of our relationship with God to the place of pure faith, surrender, and availability. We are moving below the words, beneath the "I need, I ask, I want." In the stillness we are disciplining our hearts and minds to dwell in a posture that primarily asserts, "I trust, I believe." We are learning to dwell in God's eternal "I Am." In this form of prayer we come before God fully as we are and we lean into the silence, cultivating an interior sense of knowing that God has our best intentions at heart and that we can fully and completely trust that. We are placing ourselves in the presence of God with no expectations and no demands. This, of course, is the work of the Spirit who helps us in all ways to connect to the mystery of God.

The movement that is most difficult here is the denial of self and the detachment from our thoughts (and even maybe from our desires) in order that something happen during our time of prayer. Back when I began this practice under the guidance of a spiritual director, I would wake early and go to the chair where I would follow the instructions from Keating's book faithfully. After a month or so I returned to my spiritual director and in my youthful zeal for God I complained that "nothing was happening." She smiled and gently asked me what I had hoped would happen. I replied that I was hoping God would show up, or that I would feel something different, enlightened, or wiser. Again, she smiled and invited me to stay with the practice until I no longer had an expectation for how God should act, or how I should feel. Even here we can see the undermining power of expectation as a contradiction to gratitude and awareness.

My director invited me to consider this practice as *an offering to God, a sacrifice of time and attention.* Those words captured my heart. That one sentence helped me to shift internally from making this practice about me, to making it about God. If we truly want to hear from God, to live and move and have our being in God, we will need to offer God our full attention and then be quiet enough to hear what God wants to say, even if God chooses to say nothing at all. Our stillness before God is our gift to God, and a gift to ourselves. Finally, beneath all the chatter, cacophony of impulses, fears, and desires, we can hear the holy within. The practice of centering prayer is one in which we can cultivate that rich sense of the holy in and around us. Keating likens it to cultivating our awareness not only of the river flow of thoughts and ideas that surround us constantly, but at last coming into relationship with the source of the river itself.[6] A guide for beginning this practice is offered in the sample exercises section of this chapter.

God longs for us to "be still and know" the goodness, the provision, and the very presence of God. When we take time to create a practice of attention and awareness of the Divine we are naturally led into gratitude. That is not to say there will not be stumbling blocks, challenges, or obstacles on our journey, but that the destination is one of confidence and praise. The rhythm of these two movements, first from gratitude to attention and presence, and second from attention and presence to gratitude, is like the tides of the ocean ever flowing in and out in a healing soothing pattern of life.

SAMPLE EXERCISES

Centering Prayer

Begin with choosing a time and place to practice. Choose a place where you will not be distracted and can sit comfortably for up to half an hour. Begin by settling into your body and then choose a sacred word that expresses your intention of opening and surrendering to God. Introduce that word into your imagination silently. As you become aware that you are drifting into thoughts or mentally wandering, gently reintroduce the sacred word to call yourself back. Gentleness is key here. The sacred word is not a mantra or a chant, but a way of directing your attention back to God and making yourself available for whatever God desires. Some have found it helpful to have a very gentle chime set at regular intervals to call us back to focusing on God. Each time you call yourself back with your sacred word remember that you are simply consenting to be present with the One who loves you more than you can ask or imagine. Begin with a period of fifteen to twenty minutes each day. Very helpful resources for this practice can be found at www.contemplativeoutreach.org.

Gratitude Journal and Examen

One of the most powerful ways we can begin to redirect our attention to God is to bring what is unconscious into consciousness. A tried and true way of doing that is by writing. To begin this practice, choose a journal that will be dedicated to the purpose of writing down the things for which you are most grateful. Then choose a time of day that you will dedicate to this practice. Some people find it helpful to wake early and begin the day by listing out all of the things they consider blessings: health, safety, a good night's sleep, food enough, bird song; or particular gifts: the baby's laughter, the fragrance of tea, the light as it comes into the room. Take notice of all the things that come to you as gifts from the Holy One. List as many as you can, and then re-read your list and allow the awareness of God's love, provision, and abundance to fully take up residence within you. Make space during your day to reconnect with that sensation of God's generous provision for you.

Related to this practice of keeping a gratitude journal is another ancient practice called the Examen. Traditionally, this was a practice done before bed each evening; it involves taking a few moments to look back over the day to see where you were most available to God and most touched by God's presence. We might begin simply by asking the question, "Where did I notice God's presence today?" and take time to listen within or write down what comes to mind. A slow and gentle review of the day leads us to become aware of the many graced moments that surround us. Things we might have taken for granted or not even noticed at all can become powerful experiential evidence of the God who accompanies us always. As we slowly review our day we can begin to see God beside us in all things: the conversations at work, playing in the park with the kids, or even walking through the grocery store. We might even begin to see that the plant we thought was dead has now sprouted new leaves, and suddenly we realize that God is truly calling new life out of all creation.

This expansion of our attention towards God can also be a means of inviting God to open our awareness of ourselves and how we move through our days. Self-knowledge is a challenge for all of us since we are masters of hiding behind the self we want to present to the world. As we deepen our awareness of the loving presence of God alongside of us each day, we can courageously begin to ask God to show us the place where we were faithful, and where we missed an opportunity to respond and share that love with others. We might also ask God to make us aware of attitudes, resistances, and ways in which we have not yet fully allowed God to lead our lives. Observing the missed opportunities, or encountering the stubborn parts of ourselves might fill us with disappointment or regret, but it can also make space in our imaginations to make different choices next time. This is not about making a tally sheet of successes and failures, this is about reviewing the day with the One who created and loves us and longs for us to dwell fully in that love. This practice is about opening one's heart and mind to allow God to fully reveal and illuminate the daily events of our lives.

Once you have prayerfully walked through the day simply release it to God. There is no need to carry anything forward. You can let the day's own troubles and graces be sufficient for the day. Further information and guidance on this practice can be found at www.ignatian spirituality.com.

In Your Own Words

For this practice you are invited to transpose a psalm of gratitude into your own voice and experience. Find a place where you can be still and set aside a time when you will be undisturbed. You will need a Bible and a writing utensil. You can do this practice on a weekly basis, or even daily. It is an extended version of the Examen detailed above. Begin in prayer, asking God to allow you to see God's hand in your life and to deepen your sense of appreciation and joy. Gently read through the psalm you have chosen several times and allow its cadence to dwell in you. Then copy it out substituting your own words out of the review of your week naming the goodness God has shown to you.

You can do a longer version of this exercise on a retreat or day of prayer. In the longer version you will be looking back over your whole life, or perhaps the last year, with an eye to the movement of God and the moments that are worthy of praise. Begin by taking some time in silence to review some of the most important moments in your life. Slowly and prayerfully walk through your memories of childhood. What do you remember as highlights? Were there painful moments in which God might have been present although hidden? You might take a piece of paper and draw a line and mark off decades and then outline the moments where you felt particularly blessed. Often these moments of blessing are preceded by a season of challenge or hardship. Be gentle with yourself as you walk this memory path.

Setting Up a Gratitude Altar

This exercise is based on the book, *Reminders of God: Altar for Personal and Family Devotion*, by Anne Grizzle. Choose a small space in your home you will be able to see and visit regularly. It is quite possible that you already have begun such a collection of treasures that remind you of precious times, favorite memories, and significant learnings. This exercise is about being even more conscious about creating a space to hold items that serve as reminder of some of the many ways in which God has blessed you. You can begin by culling your home for these items. Photos, natural objects, poems, and scripture passages are all great options for your gratitude altar. Some people choose to place a candle there, or a special cloth underneath. Others add incense to heighten the senses. There is no right or wrong way to create such a space. The goal is to create a visual invitation to yourself to see the ways in which God has been present in your life and to give thanks. Feel free to add and subtract the items as the Spirit moves you and as new celebrations occur in your life.

FOR FURTHER READING

Chittister, Joan and Rowan Williams. *Uncommon Gratitude*. Collegeville, MN: Liturgical Press, 2010.

De Mello, Anthony. *Sadhana: A Way to God*. New York: Doubleday/Image, 1984.

Edwards, Tilden. *Living Simply Through the Day: Spiritual Survival in a Complex Age*. New Jersey: Paulist Press, 1998.

Edwards, Tilden. *Living In the Presence*. New York: HarperCollins, 1995.

Grizzle, Ann. *Reminders of God: Altar for Personal and Family Devotion*. Brewster, MA: Paraclete Press, 2004.

Keating, Thomas. *Open Heart Open Mind: The Contemplative Dimension of the Gospel*. New York: The Continuum Publishing Company,1995.

Merton, Thomas. *Contemplative Prayer*. New York: Doubleday. 1996.

Steindl-Rast, David. *Gratefulness: The Heart of Prayer*. New York: Paulist, 1984

Voskamp, Ann. *One Thousand Gifts: A Dare to Live Fully Right Where You Are*. Grand Rapids: Zondervan, 2010.

Chapter 3

❧

Sacred Narrative: The Practice of Storytelling

When the great Rabbi Israel Baal Shem-Tov saw misfortune threatening the Jews, it was his custom to go to a certain part of the forest to meditate. There he would light a fire, say a special prayer, and the miracle would be accomplished and the misfortune averted. Later, when his disciple had occasion, for the same reason, to intercede with heaven, he would go to the same place in the forest and say: "Master of the Universe, listen! I do not know how to light the fire, but I am still able to say the prayer." And the miracle was accomplished.

Much later, another rabbi in turn, in order to save his people once more, would go into the forest and say, "I do not know how to light the fire, I do not know the prayer, but I know the place, and this must be sufficient." It was sufficient and the miracle was accomplished.

Then it fell to Rabbi Israel of Rizhyn to overcome misfortune. Sitting in his armchair, his head in his hands, he spoke to God. "I am unable to light the fire and I do not know the prayer; I cannot even find the place in the forest. All I can do is to tell the story, and this must be sufficient."
And it was sufficient.

God made people because God loves stories.
Elie Wiesel, "The Gates of the Forest"

The Miracle of Stories

Stories are the inevitable companions of people bounded by birth and death and who know it. As we stumble to speak of the ambiguity of our human relationship to Mystery, a story helps us deal with the paradox of a God who is beyond knowing yet chooses to know us.[1] A story is a way of seeing in the dark, of making some sense of the mystery of existence, of recognizing ourselves.

Stories are not so much about facts as about truths. A story uncovers and offers *meaning* in experience, organizing events by resonance and intuition rather than by analysis and mastery. Stories involve the selection of events as somehow important, and the discovery of previously unseen connections. Not everything can be said, and some things are more readily suggested. Emily Dickinson's insistence that we tell things "slant" hints at the truth that some things are better known at a glimpse than by looking at them full on.[2] The sacred reveals itself at a "slant," like the feeling of butterfly wings that brush against our cheek and are gone. When we find a way to tell our stories as people touched by the sacred, then we come close to the truth. Each story potentially mediates the mysterious and creative power of God.

Sacred scriptures are often told in the form of story. The stories in the Old Testament hold our attention: the calling of Abraham, the crossing of the Red Sea, and the testing time for the people in the wilderness. Indeed, God names himself to Moses as the One who was with Moses's forefathers in the earlier narratives, "I am the God of Abraham, Isaac, and Jacob" (Exodus 3:6). And three of the four New Testament Gospels tell the *story* of Jesus's life.

The biblical record is the story not just of God, but of the people of God, and of their relationship. The holy history/story recounted in its pages is a description, starting with the wandering Aramaean Abraham, of how Yahweh God took notice of and gradually claimed as his own the Hebrew tribes. In many ways the Bible intends to be a love story between Yahweh and his bride, Israel, the choice of one God for one people, interacting with them in the midst of their daily history, loving and forgiving them. There are noticeable patterns in the broad flow of the incidents in scripture, echoed in many of the single stories.

The Episcopal Education for Ministry program offers a pattern for these biblical stories which begins with (1) Creation, moves to (2) Sin, followed by (3) Judgment, and concluding with (4) Redemption.[3] The theological words can be simplified in a pattern involving (1) a beginning, (2) the appearance of trouble, (3) the consequences, and (4) the ultimate unfolding of unexpected new possibility. This pattern is common to many of the Hebrew people's interactions with God in the Old Testament, is echoed in the New Testament, and can be a useful way to examine any particular event or period of one's life today.

Pause to reflect:
- *Think of events in your life that might have followed this pattern; have you noticed anything like this in your life or a friend's?*
- *Is there a newspaper story or book that expresses this sequence? We often see trouble and its consequences, but how often are we aware of the emergence of new possibilities from situations that seemed hopeless?*

The escape of the Hebrews through the Red Sea is one example of this pattern in sacred story (Exodus 4:18 and following). Though they are beloved of Yahweh God (1. Creation/Beginning), the Hebrew people find themselves slaves in a foreign land. Through a series of events, the whole people have been torn from their beloved country—and have been gone so long that others have claimed their homeland *and* they themselves have become accustomed to the conditions of life as slaves to the overlords of Egypt (2. Sin/Trouble). Yahweh sends a messenger, Moses, to speak on their behalf to Pharaoh, who at first hardens his heart and refuses to release them. Through Moses, Yahweh then performs a variety of miracles, sending great suffering upon the houses of Egypt until they will let Hebrew people go. At last, Pharaoh relents, and the Hebrews hurriedly depart (3. Judgment/Consequence). But as soon as they are gone, Pharaoh changes his mind, and sends the army's chariots after them to force their return.

The Hebrews are camped by the sea when they see the Egyptian chariots drawing near, and they fear greatly. But Moses, guided by Yahweh, lifts up his staff, stretches out his hand over the sea and divides it, so that the Hebrews can pass through the sea on dry ground. A great cloud appears which holds the army back while the whole people pass through the walls of water on either side. When they are safely across, the chariots pursue, only to be drowned by the returning sea. And the Hebrew people see and marvel that God has done this great work for them (4. Redemption/Unexpected New Life).

The pattern revealed in scripture can be common to all life experience. Born in God's love, we go along day by day, and one day realize that we are in trouble. Recognition that all is not well can be understood as an invitation to cooperate in changing things. If we respond, we may find ourselves in the midst of struggle and conflict, which may even seem to make things worse in the short term, but when we look back we can recognize the evidence of the sacred in the midst of the struggle. Reflecting on the difference between now and then, we can even recognize how Love has won on our behalf. Seeing life in this way is not easy; it takes time and effort to notice and remember clearly. We are helped to notice such subtle but ever-present victories when we are familiar with the sacred stories of a faith community, which give us healing patterns we can receive and look for within our own experience.

I saw this pattern in my own life. I was employed in a bureaucracy where I had found satisfaction over the years, but was increasingly restless and uncomfortable with my current situation. I decided to make a change, moving back to the community where I felt most at home, and accepting my first job in private enterprise. My new employers suggested I work on commission, which felt a little scary but seemed a good challenge. Within eighteen months in the new job, I had made a great deal of money by my standards. I used that money to quit work and attend seminary full time, a prospect which had not even occurred to me eighteen months prior. But not until I spoke about it with my spiritual director several years later was I able to see the truth he pointed out: God had helped me make the transition for which I longed, not only by helping me find a way to leave the first job, but by giving me, in the second position, both time and money to make the shift to my true vocation. God had "saved" me, no less than the Hebrews had been saved at the Red Sea. By this example, I don't mean to suggest that God always answers prayer in this way (there have been many times for me when it didn't happen!), but that God is always with us, bringing forth good, even sometimes as a surprise.

John Shea observes that "We are the story God tells. Our very lives are the words that come from God's mouth. This insight has always fired the religious imagination. . . . The perennial Christian strategy is: (a) gather the folks, (b) break the bread, and (c) tell the stories."[4] Hearing the words, "Long ago . . . " or "Once upon a time . . . " an expectancy builds within us, so much do we love a good story, even or perhaps especially in its repetition.

Impediments to Narrative

In our own time, we seem not to understand that the core stories, the meta-patterns of the culture, are of necessity always in a process of change, if they are to remain vital. The basic story is handed over from one time and place to another, *interpreted by* the lives lived by those who pass the story along. Indeed, the word "tradition" means to hand over, expecting that the essential core is transmitted *as it has been understood and lived by those who give it*. It is expected that those who receive will likewise make adjustments necessary for their own good fit, and then also pass along what they have come to know in their living with the values they received. Such handing over carries the obligation that each one in the sequence uses discernment in determining what is most important and what needs to change. But it is only when this faithful "handing" occurs throughout the generations that the core story attains the shining patina which is the mark of its power and beauty. It is chiefly when people are no longer actively interacting with the core stories that those stories begin to lose their resilience, become rigid, and seem no longer to have any relevance to the times.

In fact, Richard Kearney points out that "There has been much talk as we pass into the third millennium that we have reached the end of the story. . . . For many people, the old Master Narratives are no longer engaging our imagination and belief."[5] Computers and the internet have fundamentally challenged those forms of remembrance presumably handed down seamlessly from one generation to the next. In a global world where information is instantly shared between and among many cultures, the old stories are giving way to new ones, more multiplotted, multivocal, and multimedia. The universe no longer seems quite as stable, coherent, continuous, and certainly not univocal. If narrative is conceived as existing only within the parameters of reductive scientism, then perhaps it is indeed dead. But if the very act of telling a good story involves nuanced skills and arts capable of engaging the Mystery surrounding us, the critics—starting from a suspicious and cynical stance—will inevitably be blind to something essential.

The problem emerges in the nature of the story itself. Is the story we tell an "open" story or a "closed" story?[6] All stories endeavor to find meaning in existence, but a closed story is one that has been so codified over time that it no longer carries any tension or dynamic energy. Closed stories are so predictable, so much settled into a past time, that they have lost their ability to evoke a spiritual response. Closed stories are reliable and soothing in their stability, but they carry no tension, no challenges. As one of the prayers bids, "Deliver us from the presumption of coming to this (Sacrament) for solace only and not for strength."[7] Closed stories are "the lifeless accounts of persons who want assurance" in contrast to the open stories of those who find themselves compelled to wrestle imaginatively with the disharmonies of existence.[8]

In contrast, an open story is a narrative that remains imaginatively developing, capable of accompanying us into the unknown, because it continuously bears the tension of "what is" and "what might be." For example, Aristotle praises the great Greek tragedies *because they evoke pity and fear*, pity for the actors in the play, and fear that our lives may one day be like theirs.[9] We are touched to the core by an open story, a story so near to experience that we know it could be our very own. There is always more to be said in a narrative that is open, because it flourishes in ambiguity. This is what gives story its unique capacity to deal with paradox and to support us as we move into the unknown future.[10]

Contemporary story-telling contains both closed and open stories, but we can teach ourselves to tell and prefer to hear/read open stories, ones that vitally touch our lives. As we practice narrative, let us endeavor to use our hearts as well as our minds, our intuition as well as our devotion, our uncertainties and pains as well as our hopes. Rather than depend on traditional tellings of our sacred stories, we may learn to encounter the stories of our traditions in a new way, seeing the old stories as ways the ancients chose in their own time to face the ambiguity of existence. The old traditions need not be discarded as closed stories, if we come to them with openness.

William Franke suggests that the way to approach a story openly is to explore a sacred text in such a way that *we ourselves become interpreted by it*.

> The word of God is not interpreted—it interprets! That is to say, it is indeed the word (himself) rather than the word (which we read), but since we are in the embarrassing position of being unable to lay hold of that word, we can only permit it to lay hold of us. (Now as we read scripture, we understand it) as the effort to allow God to address us through the medium of the text.[11]

Thus sacred stories—as told, or as read—can be understood as involving vulnerability and a willingness to be changed by what we read, truly open to the ongoing possibilities they permit.

Sacred Reading

One of the oldest Christian practices is a way of sacred reading, a practice widely used in Benedictine monasteries to read scripture, called *lectio divina,* literally "reading divinely" (and usually pronounced *leksio*). Benedict, who founded the communities that bear his name in sixth century Italy, begins his *Regula* (Rule) for monastics with these words: "Listen with the ear of your heart, my beloved, to the words of one who loves you." Then Benedict calls upon members of the monastic communities to spend *four hours per day in lectio divina!* Known for his brevity of speech, Benedict spent no further time describing the practice, and over time, the art was lost.

Today, much of our reading of scripture is information-based, seeking to comprehend exactly what is being said, based on contemporary abilities to date textual materials, to compare our scriptures with other written materials of the time, and so forth. *Lectio* is at variance with such practices, and is actually more akin to the way early Christians would have read their contemporaries known as "the Fathers," that is, such Christians as Hilary, Ambrose, Augustine of Hippo, some of whom are introduced in the text box in this chapter. In those first early centuries, the leaders of the church were acutely aware that the words of scripture were full of mystery, with a power in the inspired word that transcended the overt purpose or meaning of a particular text.[12] Sacred reading speaks not only to an author's (past) moments of inspiration, but also to the present situation of the reader. The word is believed to open an actual encounter with the Holy, enabling the reader to turn to scripture with expectancy and eagerness.

Susan Muto makes clear that "sacred reading is an art requiring us to develop attitudes more or less different from those required for informational reading."[13] She distinguishes between the attitude of *digging* for answers in informational reading, in contrast to sacred reading's *dwelling* on life meanings that may light up for us in the text. Other distinctions are dialectical/comparative assessment in contrast to docility to the text at hand, and dissective/analytical in contrast to a dynamic discovery of connections to our own life here and now.

The early Fathers believed that the overall sense of Scripture included the (1) literal/historical (the most basic level of understanding what is written) but they advised that one must go more deeply into what they called (2) the allegorical sense, which initially meant interpreting the passage as an example or hint of Christ to come. Today, this level of understanding more often refers to a metaphorical sense, the way images or metaphors are used to suggest more than the literal. Next is (3) the moral or behavioral sense, showing us how we are expected to behave in relation to what we read, and finally (4) the anagogical or mystical sense; the way in which the passage brings us into contact with hope for the future, and hopefully a keen sense of God's direct presence.[14]

John Cassian, a monk of the Egyptian desert in the third century, gives us an example to help us understand this ancient Christian practice, using the single word "Jerusalem," which appears often in the Bible. It may be taken in four senses: (1) literally/historically, as the city of the Jews; (2) allegorically/metaphorically as the Church of Christ; (3) morally/behaviorally as the human soul, which is frequently subject to praise or blame from the Lord under this term; and (4) anagogically/mystically as the heavenly city of God, which is both our mother and our goal.[15]

I find it helpful to stay with a text for a while, giving an author the benefit of the doubt regarding what might have been intended that might also touch me. For example, in reading and praying with the *Rule of St. Benedict*, I am initially inclined to avoid his references to Psalm 137:9, in which the Israelite psalmist expresses hope that the Babylonian babies might be dashed to death on the rocks before they had a chance to grow up and become oppressors like their fathers. Benedict alludes to this offensive passage twice in his *Rule*, and I find it horrific (RB Prologue 28 and RB 4:50), but I stay with the text for a time, recalling that Benedict probably had prayed this Biblical text metaphorically, initially realizing that "rock" is a term often applied to God in Christ. From there, it is not too great a stretch to imagine that "things in their infancy" could refer to temptations in their earliest stages, which are to be offered to the rock of Christ at once, rather than allowing them to gain a foothold in the mind and heart (the moral meaning). Finally, because we can trust Christ's gift of unconditional love, even and beyond the cross, we can also be assured we are fully able to deal with temptations arising now and even in the future (the mystical meaning). The point is that the practice of sacred reading gives us an openness to find deep and direct meanings in texts which otherwise might seem completely unfruitful.

Some sections of scripture lend themselves more readily to *lectio* than others. In general, good choices include stories, parables, and verses with strong action or concrete images. Further, *lectio* blossoms when working with short passages, perhaps four verses or so at a time, re-reading them again and again, each time allowing one's heart to expand receptively to the Word. A commitment to the practice of *lectio* with scripture or other spiritual readings prospers if one sets aside a regular time for it, in a space where one can rest undisturbed. Begin by releasing other thoughts and concerns and seeking inner silence; then stay with it for a previously determined period (say, three to six months, once or twice a week) even through times when we don't sense much happening. It might be well to keep a reflective reading notebook, jotting a few notes after each session, to which you may wish to return from time to time.

The overall *process* of lectio may be summarized as reflection on three questions: (1) what does the passage say? (2) what does it say to me? and (3) what does it say to me to be and to do? Fundamentally this pattern of reading can be usefully applied both to scripture and to spiritual reading. You may find more detail about sacred reading in several books mentioned at the end of this chapter. Some of the Christian spiritual classics are noted in the text box, which may offer you a good place to start on sacred reading beyond the scriptures themselves.

Christian Spiritual Classics

Note: There are many of these classics, and the suggestions under Overview of Spiritual Classics at the end of this chapter offer short selections of some, and a guide to selecting others. These represent my/our top picks, more or less historical in order.

Roberta C. Bondi, *To Love as God Loves: Conversations with the Early Church.* A great help in understanding the desert Fathers and Mothers.

John Cassian, *Conferences.* A readable account of many interviews with early desert Christians.

Bede, *A History of the English Church and People.* Early monastic life in England.

Gregory of Nyssa, *The Life of Moses.* Interprets Moses's interactions with God.

Augustine of Hippo, *Confessions*, and *Sermons.* Major source of Western spiritual thought, both Catholic and Protestant.

Benedict of Nursia, *Rule.* I recommend my devotional commentary on this, *Preferring Christ.*

Bernard of Clairvaux, *On Loving God*. Insights on deepening prayer.
Hildegard of Bingen. I particularly like Matthew Fox's commentary called
Illuminations.
Anonymous, *The Cloud of Unknowing*. A favorite of mystics.
Julian(a) of Norwich, *Revelations of Divine Love*. Conviction that all shall be
well, set in the midst of a suffering world.
Teresa of Avila, *Interior Castle*. Deep exploration of stages in the life of
prayer.
Ignatius of Loyola, *Exercises*. Overview of a spiritual retreat by the Jesuit
author who has influenced much American spirituality.
Francis de Sales, *Introduction to the Devout Life*. Help in prayer and living
a spiritual life.
John Calvin, *Writings on Pastoral Piety*. One of the major leaders of the
Reformation.
Martin Luther, *Spirituality*. We cannot "work" for Grace, which is a free
gift.
Anonymous, *The Way of the Pilgrim*. A beautiful primer on constant prayer:
"Jesus: Mercy!"

And few contemporary folks (anything they write):

Wilkie Au
Ruth Burrows
Joan Chittister
Anthony deMello
Anne LaMott
Thomas Merton
Philip Newall
Henry Nouwen
John O'Donahue
Richard Rohr
Joyce Rupp
Joseph Schmidt
Jean Vanier

Finally, I haven't listed publishers, because many of these books are
published by several. I do recommend Paulist Press' Classics of Western
Spirituality.

The Stories of Our Lives

Recall that this chapter began stating that God made humans because
God loves stories. And our stories are not just stories of God, but also
importantly stories about our own lives. Some of us may feel that our

lives are fragmented, with a portion here and a portion there, but no glue between. What continuity might exist? What connections might there be between where we have been and where we are going? It may seem we have no true center, no true importance. Probably all of us experience that occasionally. The ongoing discovery of what our personal story is all about is central to the deepening of our spiritual lives. Simply to have a life is not to have a story. Yet, if each of us is indeed God's beloved, indeed in relationship with God, then we have an emerging sacred story, whether we are aware of it or not! Our story helps us gain a sense of our unique specialness. We come to know ourselves as loved for just exactly who we are, believing that God's call to each of us is fundamentally the statement, "I rejoice that you exist." As we begin to find ways to tell our personal story, let us remember we do it to learn to see ourselves in God's eyes — not so much in terms of our sins, as more importantly in terms of our potential.

As a start, try this exercise. Settle into silence, and ask yourself, "When did the present time in my life begin?" There is no "right" answer, just whatever seems good to you today. Set aside that awareness for now.

Then take a piece of blank paper, and divide the years of your life up until this present time into three main periods. Again, there is no right answer, just what you think and feel now. Name each period. For *each* of them, answer these four questions:

1. What was I searching/hoping for in that period?
2. What did I find in that period?
3. Who was God for me then?
4. Who was I for God then?

When you have answered these questions, sit back and reflect on what you have written. Do any new insights emerge for you? After a time, if you wish, you may answer the same four questions for the "present time" in your life. I have done this exercise many times, and my answers are somewhat different each time. I find it a very useful way to begin thinking about my life's sacred story and allowing it to unfold further.

Reflection on Life

Reflection on life is one primary method to begin our personal story. When we return later quietly to consider life happenings, we can deepen our discovery of how they are penetrated by the sacred. Reflection doesn't mean hindsight or the endless hashing over something we said or did, wishing that it had been different. Nor is reflection meant as a substitute for first-hand reality, the total experience of being alive in the moment. Rather, reflection is spiritually complementary to events, as a later review of experience in a gentle and open way, anticipating that we will discover more in the event than we knew at the time, with the help of the Holy Spirit.

Experiences happen. In the midst of any occurrence, it is difficult to be wholly aware of all that is taking place. Although we can teach ourselves to increase our awareness and attention in the actual moment, experience itself can be greatly enriched by calling it back to mind at a later time, reflecting upon it at leisure. When we attend to anything carefully, it reveals the presence of the sacred within. This is not something that most of us have learned. We tend to give attention to things seeking their function, analyzing them into component parts, demanding they reveal their usefulness to us. Reflection is a quality of presence to our life experience that enables us to become newly aware of mystery and holiness not seen before.

Reflection is what I call *lectio on life*, because it brings us back again and again to that deep attentiveness which is receptivity to the Holy. To find the sacred in all, it is not sufficient to take a quick glance at the most literal level. One must continue to be present with levels of awareness, moving deeper and deeper into communion with whatever it is, until we see it with God's own eyes.

The "method" of reflection is so simple that it seems disarming. Below I describe how it might go, in an example from my life.

1. Life happens; an incident occurs.
2. We reflect on that incident, by bringing it back consciously to mind and "listening" to it.
   - First, we recall the physical details as vividly as possible: what were the sights and sounds, the colors, the smells, and how did events unfold in time? *One afternoon, my husband and I planned to visit my cousin and his wife on the other side of town. We drove up on the sidewalk in front of his house, and they were in their front yard, working on the lawn. My cousin and wife were in "grubby" clothes of the sort worn while doing heavy work. He held a rake, and she some sort of shovel. The lawn was yellow in the early spring, and they were clearly planning to spend the afternoon getting the soil restored and ready for the summer, even though*

we'd made the date ahead of time. Doug and I got out of the car and walked over to them, and they neither raised their heads from their work nor greeted us. For now in reflection, I don't let myself get into the emotions of the event, but just concentrate on the physical setting.

- Second, we explore what we and others brought to the incident, looking particularly at any point where feelings or energy markedly shifted. As we reflect now on what occurred, we may become aware of something not noticed at the time or newly emerging now. *For some time my cousin and I had been at odds, for reasons not entirely clear to me. As children, we'd been close, but in recent years, it had been painful to see him because I felt so rejected by him. Nevertheless, we had kept up a pretense of civility. I was not particularly aware of anything new in our situation, so I was surprised by their lack of hospitality. We stood on the lawn, chatting awkwardly for a few minutes, until I said something that set him off. He shouted at me, and told me how awful I was. I think I shouted something back, before Doug and I got in the car and drove home, with me crying all the way. As I reflected on the incident, I realized that the moment when the energy really shifted, when I really fell apart, was when I felt so judged by him. That happened so often when we were together that I felt nothing I could do would please him. Reflecting and letting myself move more deeply into that moment, it occurred to me that I also was judging him. I felt that so much about his lifestyle and attitudes were wrong, and I realized that without doubt he felt my judgment. It had not previously occurred to me that it was a two-way street.* If we gain some new insight, we make a commitment to let that insight become part of our subsequent experience. If no new material comes, we relax with that.

- Third, when we have gone as far as possible in replaying the event without judgment, with a deep breath we release everything about it, as fully as we can. In imagination, we hand everything over to the Holy One; letting it go into greater hands than ours. However incomplete or unresolved or frustrated we feel about the incident, we give it away for now. *My insight gave me a whole new perspective on what had been going on between us. With God so present in my reflections, I had been able to see my part in the problem without becoming immediately defensive. With thanksgiving, I offered our relationship up to God, trusting that*

God would continue to help me deal with it in future by being present to both of us.

- Fourth and finally, we go on with our lives, taking the next best step we can. *I promised myself that right now, I would begin working to let go of my judgment of my cousin, and try very hard to act accordingly at our next meeting.*

In reflection we become more deeply aware of the presence of the sacred within life experience. But how does this happen? When we set aside the time and space to be present to anything, not to judge nor analyze, but rather to be receptive and expectant, elements emerge to our vision of which we were previously unaware. The sacred is not a commodity that can be produced upon demand, but is in some ways more like a shy, wild thing which only visits the one willing to wait in stillness. When we faithfully continue the process of reflection, life begins to present more surprises and more gifts. Although *cumulatively* reflection can shift a whole life's direction, it usually does not bring about immediate and dramatic change. Rather the effects seem to come more in periodic increments, which in time are profoundly transforming.

Usually it is well to start the practice of reflection with something simple, such as an encounter with an unpleasant (or pleasant) salesperson, helping a stranger, disappointing a friend, being struck by an article in the daily news, or the completion of a long-overdue report. Beginning gradually with relatively minor but engaging events of a normal day, we practice reflection on experiences that are not loaded with heavy feelings. But there will undoubtedly come a time when we will want to reflect upon memories of troublesome and painful events that are pivotal to our lives. If these are major and unhealed matters, it is often good to obtain the help and insights of someone other than ourselves, perhaps a spiritual director or a professional therapist, who can see more clearly than we. But even counseling may not be enough to give us a sense of how these difficulties contribute to the whole story of our lives. How do sorrow, grief, and loss contribute to our stories without dominating them?

Our Own Sacred Stories

In dealing with issues such as these, we may find that the meta-stories from scripture and myth are useful sources to supplement our own experience. If our only reference points are the boundaries of our personal lives, then losses and suffering can indeed seem tragic and overwhelmingly cruel. To say that personal pain can be a part of re-membering toward wholeness through the insights of core cultural stories is not to minimize the suffering involved. But suffering is often more bearable if we can glimpse some reason or use for it, or remember similar situations in our core stories.

A "sacred" story is any story that reveals the reality of God. Normally such stories involve trouble or crisis because that is the human experience. From the outside, or in later reflection, we may be able to see an undesirable event as an opportunity for new life, but new life always requires a kind of dying to something of what was, so the choice is genuinely difficult. However hard, crisis often brings with it the power to choose. In sacred space, the one who reflects discovers that embedded in what is, is More Than she had known. And the More Than is not just outside, but embedded within one's own being. The "More Than," the Mystery, is both abiding and empowering. But we need to see it and believe in its effectiveness. God is elusive and intangible, but our traditions and experience make clear that God's life is interwoven with our own. Learning and telling our own sacred stories is about discovering wholeness in our midst and then choosing to embrace the possible future.

SAMPLE EXERCISES

1. Start playfully by asking questions of yourself.
   (a) Imagine that you are a vegetable or an animal: at this moment, what would you be and why?
   (b) Think of a metaphor to describe a challenge you recently faced: it was like a . . . what?
   (c) What was the best holiday you ever had?

2. Write an autobiography of prayer. At various periods in your life, what was your prayer like? Have there been periods when you felt a little "superstitious," say, that if you "stepped on a crack," a dire result would occur? Did you ever deal with God as if a "vending machine," believing that if you "pushed a certain button," you would get just the result you wanted? Was there a period of utter trust and devotion? Did life events ever suggest that a certain form

of prayer was or was not reliable? Do you have a sense of what you would hope for your prayer to be like in the near future?

3. Make a "map" of your soul country. Using a large blank piece of paper and colored pens or pencils, think about a geographic metaphor for yourself. Are you a continent, an island, a small nation surrounded by others? What do your boundaries look like, and what is adjacent to them? Are there cities and farms scattered around? Play with it for a time, decide if there's something you'd like to change or add, and consider what images were "given" to you as you worked.

4. Consider two questions and journal on your thoughts:
   (a) What is dying in me at present?
   (b) What is birthing in me at present?

FOR FURTHER READING

Story

Urban T. Holmes III. *Ministry and Imagination*. New York: Seabury, 1981.
Richard Kearney. *On Stories*. New York: Routledge, 2002.
John Shea. *Stories of God: An Unauthorized Biography*. Chicago: Thomas More Press, 1978.

Lectio Divina

Michael Casey. *Sacred Reading: The Ancient Art of Lectio Divina*. Ligouri, MO: Liguori/Triumph Press, 1996.
Jean Leclerq, O.S.B. *The Love of Learning and the Desire for God: A Study of Monastic Culture*. Trans. Catharine Misrahi. New York: Fordham UP, 1982.
M. Robert Mulholland, Jr. *Shaped by the Word: The Power of Scripture in Spiritual Formation*. Nashville, TN: Upper Room Books, 1985.
Christine Valters Paintner and Lucy Wynkoop, O.S.B. *Lectio Divina: Contemplative Awakening and Awareness*. Mahwah, NJ: Fortress, 2008.
Norvene Vest. *Gathered in the Word: Praying the Scripture in Small Groups*. Nashville, TN: Upper Room Books, 1996.
Elie Wiesel. *Messengers of God: Biblical Portraits & Legends* (on Midrash). Trans. Marion Wiesel. New York: Pocket Books, 1977.

Overview of Classic Spiritual Texts

David. A. Fleming, S.M., editor. *The Fire and the Cloud: An Anthology of Catholic Spirituality: Basic Writings by the Great Mystics of History*. Mahwah, NJ: Paulist Press, 1978

Richard J. Foster and James Bryan Smith, editors. *Devotional Classics: Selected Readings for Individuals and Groups.* New York: Harper, 1990.

Susan Annette Muto. *A Practical Guide to Spiritual Reading.* Revised. Petersham, MA: St. Bede's Publications, 1994.

Chapter 4

Time and Money: The Practice of Trusting God's Sufficiency

Be no more than God hath made thee.
Give over thine own willing;
Give over thine own running;
Give over thine own desiring to know or be anything,
And sink down to the seed which God sows in thy heart,
And let that grow in thee, and be in thee, and breathe in thee, and act in thee,
And thou shalt find by sweet experience
That the Lord knows that, and loves and owns that,
And will lead it to the inheritance of life, which is God's portion.
Isaac Pennington

Abundance

The opening verses of the book of Genesis are an exquisite visual symphony of call and response. Everything begins in darkness in what is described as a formless void. We are swimming in nothingness and then God calls forth light, separates it from the darkness, and a dazzling new reality emerges. Rather than an endless shadow, or perpetual day, God chose to balance all things, light and dark, day and night. In this initial act of creation, God gives us the first measure of what we will later come to call time; the passage of day into night. It is pure gift, and it is a loving way to organize the "formless void" in which we might otherwise be lost. God continues to structure and populate creation with skies, seas, vegetation, stars, and creatures. What God creates is pleasing and with each new aspect that comes forth, God blesses it and calls it good. All of creation is sufficient, and there is nothing lacking. On the seventh day, having completed this festival of phenomenal creativity, God rests. This day, this Sabbath of ceasing productivity, God blesses and calls *holy*. It is so good that it is deemed sacred. This day of rest and gratitude is set apart from the effort and flurry of activity that happens on other days. This flow of days one to another and the holy model for ceasing work one in every seven days is also a gracious gift from the Holy One—if only we are willing to receive it.

History and experience seem to show that there is some aspect of our humanness that resists receiving such gifts. Furthermore, we are still filled with desire despite the fact that we are surrounded with more than enough for our needs. If we read just one chapter further into Genesis, we see how poorly we humans do when surrounded with every possible goodness in a garden of delights and required to refrain from only one thing (see Genesis 2). We just can't seem to resist reaching for that one tree that is off limits. An undeniable aspect of our human nature is that we seem to have an inability to be satisfied with what is right before us. We deeply resist being constrained in any way. We want to be in control and tame the elements and resources around us. We create climate-controlled houses and artificial light to alter the span of time in which we can work. We save money and invest hoping for a good return. We toss and turn at night fretting and fearing that we will not have enough time or money. All the while the Holy One whispers, shouts, and sings of sufficiency. One of the greatest challenges in the spiritual life is to develop a healthy, life- giving relationship with both finances and the way in which we spend our days. To do that we will need to look at the human construct of time and begin to listen for God's call to balance. In the same way we will need to consider what God suggests is a right relationship to money.

Time

In the earliest of days, time was measured in changing moons and the flow of seasons. The appearance of the first green sprigs of spring or the final fall harvest of the crops grounded us to the Earth, to God, and to one another. We needed one another for the hunt and the growing of crops. We honored the Creator in both. Simply making it through another winter was cause for praise. It did not take long for us to try to tame the fluid passage of the days and nights into segments that could be measured. Our ancient ancestors devised sundials and ever since we have been measuring time more and more precisely. Water clocks and hourglasses broke the sacred steady flow into pieces that we could now pretend to possess, barter with, and ultimately come to fret over their imagined insufficiency. Time is now used as a construct to call us to market, limit lawyers' debates, and help us keep watch in the night. The old saying, *Your time has run out*, is based in the sands in the hourglass falling to mark a set period of time for debate in the Roman era, and now carries an even deeper sense of foreboding. What began as God's abundant provision is now distorted with our belief that time is scarce. The practice of honoring God with our attention to time is an invitation to restore our sense of abundance and goodness in God's rhythm of creation.

It is the rare person who feels they have enough time to do all that they wish to do. This myth of scarcity is rampant. Modern, first world cultures are increasingly driven by productivity and making every second count. With time of the essence, we race to a nearby fast food restaurant for lunch, where the average meal takes about eleven minutes. At home, many parents confess that they spend twice as much time answering emails as playing with or talking to their children. They reach for the now popular, and very efficient, one-minute bedtime stories. Even play time is shrinking, with whole games taking less than ninety seconds on portable electronics. With each new invention hailed as a time saver, we learn that the baseline of expectations for response times or home cleanliness is only raised and thus we are stuck on the wheel of endlessly increasing expectations.

In the mid-1980s, the Japanese began to notice that numerous top executives were dropping dead with no prior indications of poor health. The word *Karoshi*, death from overwork, entered the vocabulary of the world and stands as a haunting reminder of what can happen if our lives fall out of balance. In this modern era, the psalmist's call is as urgent as ever, "Teach us to number our days, that we may gain a wise heart" (Psalm 90:12). Placing our days before the Holy One, inviting God to direct and gently fill these numbered days is a way forward into gracious balance. Actively making space for appreciation and dwelling in the presence of holy mystery, taking time for rest, play, and contemplation, in addition to the tasks that are asked of us, adds equilibrium.

Keeping Sabbath—Redeeming Time

From the creation story we receive God's model of balance in resting one out of every seven days. Even God seems to need to pause and be still and appreciate creation. Our need for this God-given Sabbath rhythm moves front and center with Moses and the Hebrews' exodus from Egypt. In that story we learn of the miraculous escape and the subsequent formation of an identity as the people of God. Central to the community's identity, as laid out in the Ten Commandments, is the keeping of the Sabbath for all people. God tells us we will forget our names, forget where we are from, and forget to whom we belong if we do not pause once every seven days to remember, rest, and give thanks. God asks that we cease our work and offer God our full attention one in seven days. Keeping the Sabbath holy is a particular honoring of time that serves both as a sign of respect and gratitude to God as well as for our own wholeness and wellbeing.

This way of honoring God by ceasing work and giving my full attention became piercingly vivid for me through an interaction with my daughter. It had been another busy day at work and school for both of us, and I was trying to get dinner on the table as quickly as possible. She was telling me something important about her day, but I had my back turned to her and was vaguely nodding and listening as I chopped vegetables. I was much more preoccupied with looking at the recipe than with hearing her. Finally, she got quiet for a moment and said, "I need you to hear this; I can't tell if you are listening if you don't stop and look at me." Those words stopped me from missing what was more important than the chore, namely, relationship. I almost missed it, and she might have given up and just walked off, but by sheer grace I was able to respond to her loving invitation to be present and share in an important moment in her life. She wanted me to know who she was and to share herself with me, and I could only fully receive that gift by stopping and completely attending to her.

It is the same with God. Sabbath keeping is an invitation to stop and listen with the whole of who we are. We are invited to lean in and be named by the love that God waits to lavish on us. We only need to pause long enough to receive it. Our most limited and valuable commodity is our attention. With a Bluetooth headphone attached to our ear, and a smart phone in our hand, we are nearly drowning in voices competing for our attention. All our preoccupations leave us fragmented, and distracted, and exhausted. God's call to Sabbath is the way to wholeness, clarity of focus, and life-giving rest.

Pause to reflect:

- *What are your first thoughts about trying to take a day off and be with God?*
- *What seems most daunting about it? What seems most attractive?*
- *If you could create the perfect Sabbath day, what would it be like? Where would you go? What would you eat? Who would you be with? How would you spend time enjoying God's creation and being present to the goodness that surrounds you?*

One valuable voice in the search to reclaim the practice of Sabbath comes from Marva Dawn, theologian, author, and educator in Vancouver. Her book, *Keeping the Sabbath Wholly*, is a rich and well-written resource for anyone who wants to take seriously the practice of Sabbath keeping. Her book lifts up four primary movements in Sabbath keeping: ceasing, resting, embracing, and feasting.[1] The first movement of ceasing seems to be the most difficult for many. The majority of us allow our self-worth to be created through our work and our achievements, and we can't imagine letting go of being productive, or of not accomplishing something in a given day. It seems like a waste of a perfectly good day to just "do nothing." But the miracle is that in our ceasing, we are actually enacting a deep trust that God takes care of what needs to happen and that the world can spin without us pushing it along. By stopping work for one day, we practice claiming the goodness of creation and deepen our sense of the presence of God. Otherwise when we work seven days a week, we find ourselves back in Egypt making bricks for a new Pharaoh. But the practice of honoring the Sabbath and keeping it holy helps us face our own idolatry of being "self-made" and see that we are not, in fact, God. As we stop work on the Sabbath, we are also called to stop worrying. Jesus reminds us of God's gracious provision in Matthew's gospel when he invites the disciples to take a look around them and see that the lilies of the field are clothed without effort and stress, and the birds of the air are fed without anxiety. We can trust that God knows what we need, and that God has our best interest at heart (Matthew 6:25-30).

After ceasing, we are invited to rest. Allowing our bodies, minds, and spirits to settle into the arms of the Holy One is a sacred practice. On a recent retreat, I had the lovely experience of swinging in a hammock for the better part of an afternoon. I admired the flow of the wind in the trees, listened to bird song, drifted in and out of a nap. It was truly holy. As I allowed myself to let go more fully into God, a verse from an old hymn by Isaac Watts began to sing within me, "There would I find a settled rest, while others go and come, no more a stranger, nor a guest, but like a child at home."[2] This is the invitation of Sabbath; to rest and remember that we are children of God and to savor all the good gifts we have been given. We truly do not need to strive, grasp, or push, only be still and savor the goodness that already surrounds us.

Embracing and feasting follow in Dawn's marvelous outline for Sabbath. Traditional Sabbaths would be centered on a celebratory meal enjoyed with close friends and family. The benefits of such a gathering are numerous, from the joy of simply being together, to savoring tradition and expressing gratitude. Perhaps not surprisingly, emerging research indicating that children who enjoy table rituals with parents are less likely to smoke, drink, or use illicit drugs adds another powerful motivator to gather and hold that time sacred even if an entire day of Sabbath cannot be observed.[3]

My own practice in Sabbath keeping was slow to start. As a young mother with a longing to be closer to God, I knew that I wanted this luxurious restorative experience too. I set about preparing to keep the Sabbath. I blocked off time, gathered the books I wanted, prepared meals ahead of time and got ready to savor. My sense of calm and lack of productivity lasted exactly an hour and a half that first day. The siren call of the laundry was tempting me to "get ahead." Surely God would not mind if I tossed a load of the kid's clothes in, right? And so the dance began. Always there is the temptation to just do a little something, and the desire to be productive. Deeper still is the longing to be still and honor God with all of my attention. With each chore that came to mind, which I chose not to do, I could hear God inviting me to trust that it would all get accomplished, that I could truly rest in God's grace. I discovered that attending to God on that one day deepened my awareness of God in the other days. I found when I did pick up the laundry again on Monday, I actually had gratitude for the little legs and feet that filled those socks and pants, rather than the overwhelmed resentment that often had accompanied the chore. I was renewed and ready to be laboring again.

Together, my husband and I discovered the necessity for keeping Sabbath as a clergy couple. The Sabbath practice I had started as a stay at home mother fell away in my enthusiasm as a young pastor serving a congregation. One evening as we sat down to see when we might go to the movies together, we realized that in our zeal to serve our congregations we had left not one common day off in the upcoming three months to be together. We were stunned. Weddings, retreats, and special visits had completely taken over our calendars. We vowed right then to return to claiming one day in seven as ours and God's. To say yes to keeping the Sabbath would mean saying no to other invitations and opportunities, but they did not compare with the joy of resting in God with one another. It has been challenging at times to refuse invitations and requests to join others even for the best of occasions, but it has grounded us and freed us, which is exactly what is at the heart of all Sabbath practice.

It seems important here to note that not all people are surrounded by what most of us would call goodness, or perhaps even freedom. In fact, many of the world's people live in profound suffering. The intention of inviting this Sabbath practice is to cultivate a sense of God's provision no matter what the situation in which you find yourself. There is no place where God is not present. In the refugee camps, brothels, battlefields, and the depths of addiction, God is there and God's love is available and sufficient. In fact, in these places God is perhaps even more present since God, "draws near to those who are broken hearted and saves those who are crushed in spirit" (Psalm 34:18). Even in those places of profound pain, it is possible to cease participating in the violence and pain and rest in God's love. Sabbath keeping is as much about claiming our identity as sons and daughters of the living God as it is about putting down our shovels and walking away from the keyboard once a week.

A Portion and a Pause for God

For many who are beginning to seek a deeper spiritual life, an entire day of attending only to God may seem like too big a leap and, for many who work in the service fields, it is an unheard-of luxury. If a weekly Sabbath day seems entirely beyond reach, then perhaps the practice of the Divine Office might be a doorway into the practice of letting go, if only for a few moments at set times each day. The Psalms give us some of the origins of this practice. "It is good to give thanks to the Lord, to sing praises to your name, O Most High; to declare your steadfast love in the morning, and your faithfulness by night" (Psalm 92). Early Christians kept set hours for prayer following the tradition of their Jewish heritage. Over centuries, these have grown into a set of observed times at which people across the world pause to read Scripture and pray. As we will learn in chapter 5, there are eight set times in which the faithful are called to prayer, but we might choose any one or two of them to begin our own practices of Sabbath. The intention is to allow God to enter our consciousness and to be reminded of the holiness and provision of God no matter where we are. It is a practice of letting go of our busyness and making time and space for the Holy to breathe within us. In that pause and resting, we can be graced with an awareness that God can indeed be trusted to provide for all that we need that, in fact, God's grounding and guiding love surrounds us always.

God is the Giver of All—Redeeming Money

A sense of sufficiency, and the possibility of letting go, is perhaps nowhere more difficult than in the realm of money. Adults and children alike are slow to release what they believe is theirs. Every parent of every child has heard the cry, "Mine!" when attempting to even move a valued possession. This idea of "mine" is perhaps the starting place for reflection on the Christian relationship with money. The witness of Scripture helps us understand how to have a right relationship with money. First and foremost, we learn that all of creation and every good gift, including money, belongs to God.

> "Yours, O Lord, are the greatness, the power, the glory, the victory, and the majesty; for all that is in the heavens and on earth is yours: yours is the kingdom, O Lord, and you are exalted as head above all."
> (1 Chronicles 12:11)

Becoming reconciled to this reality can be a real challenge to our identities and sense of self-worth, especially if we have come to believe that we are the source of our own good fortune. The majority of us are raised to believe that what we have worked to create belongs to us. We worked hard and earned our houses, cars, and gardens, or so we think. In that worldview, we have made ourselves the center of everything, and we have failed to see that it is truly by God's grace that we happen to be who and what we are.

As a young girl, I recall a walk around our family farm with my father. He was an avid gardener and had an orchard, berry patches, rose hedges, and various beds of lilacs and peonies. In the twilight, we liked to go see what was growing and coming into season. I marveled at the abundance and variety in bloom that evening and asked my dad, "Aren't you so proud of all that you grew and made happen here?" Without missing a beat, he simply said, "I am just the caretaker. I didn't grow this. God did and, by God's grace, I get to enjoy it and take care of it for a while." That conversation forever changed the way I have viewed everything from my homes to my children. They belong to God, and I just to get to enjoy them and take care of them for a while. When we understand ourselves as stewards of God's riches, we can begin to ask the important question of what God might want us to do with what we have been given.

While God's intention for our resources might seem like an undecipherable mystery, it is actually quite clear. One cannot read Scripture without coming to the conclusion that all that has been given to us is meant for the building up of community and the breaking down of the barriers of poverty and need. From the Exodus narrative to the first church in the book of Acts, the people of God understand that whatever has been given them by the Lord is to be shared for the well-being of all (Acts 4:32-35). In fact, this understanding of restoration and reconciliation where private property and debt is concerned is laid out quite carefully.

Just before arriving in the promised land, after wandering in the wilderness, Moses is given instructions for a year of Jubilee that includes a Sabbath for the land and the reversal of property to its original owner. It also includes cancellation of debts and a freeing of slaves (Leviticus 25). This is a radical call to surrender our sense of private ownership and achievement where property and wealth are concerned. It is an invitation to profound obedience and restoration of right relationship with fellow humans, funds, and land. One cannot help but wonder how different the world might be today if such instructions were faithfully carried out. It seems our anxiety about having enough and our fears for the future keep us from following much of what God calls us to do for our own wellbeing and the wellbeing of all of creation.

This tension and anxiety about possessions is ancient, and Jesus had much to say on the matter. In a passage found in both Matthew and Luke's gospel, Jesus is teaching before a crowd. He is aware that his message of honoring and caring for the most vulnerable and trusting God is not popular among the people or the authorities of the day. He tells the crowd that they can trust God to give them the words they will need if they are brought to trial. Just then a young man shouts out from the crowd asking Jesus to tell his brother to divide the family inheritance with him. Jesus responds with a story:

> He said to them, "Take care! Be on your guard against all kinds of greed; for one's life does not consist in the abundance of possessions." Then he told them a parable: "The land of a rich man produced abundantly. And he thought to himself, 'What should I do, for I have no place to store my crops?' Then he said, 'I will do this: I will pull down my barns and build larger ones, and there I will store all my grain and my goods. And I will say to my soul, 'Soul, you have ample goods laid up for many years; relax, eat, drink, be merry." But God said to him, 'You fool! This very night your life is being demanded of you. And the things you have prepared, whose will they be?' So it is with those who store up treasures for themselves but are not rich toward God. And do not keep striving for what you are to eat and what you are to drink, and do not keep worrying. Instead, strive for his kingdom, and these things will be given to you as well. Sell your possessions, and give alms. For where your treasure is, there your heart will be also." (Luke 12:15-35 selected verses)

What might it mean to be rich towards God as this passage suggests? Certainly it does not mean building bigger barns to store more stuff. Perhaps what is being invited is a posture of generosity toward God and toward others in God's name. It is possible to put not only our finances to work for God, but we ourselves might offer up all that we are; our interests, our talents, our gifts toward loving others as a blessing to God.

Pause to reflect:
- *Do you have things tucked away in storage? If so, do you know why you hang on to them? Is it possible that they might be donated in order to benefit a cause that might help others?*
- *What gifts or talents do you have that you might make available to God? Could you help with a local literacy project? Could you tutor young children? Could you visit folks who are homebound or deliver meals?*
- *In what ways in your life do you strive to be "rich towards God?"*

Throughout history we have been given marvelous examples of those who sought to follow the way of Christ more fully. The witness of history also shows us that we are not the first ones to struggle with the issues of possessions and simplicity. Further it can give us windows into the ways those who have come before us have navigated these waters. The Desert Fathers and Mothers have much to offer us as we reflect on possessions and relationship with God. Richard Foster helps us see the parallels of that time with our modern era.

> Their world asked, "How can I get more?" The Desert Fathers and Mothers asked, "What can I do without?" Their world asked, "How can I find myself?" The Desert Mother's and Father's asked, "How can I lose myself?" Their world asked, "How can I win friends and influence people?" The Desert Fathers and Mothers asked, "How can I love God?"[4]

What the Desert Mothers and Fathers teach us is a posture of simplicity and renunciation which are doorways to the profound freedom of the spiritual life. Think of the hours and energy spent organizing, cleaning, worrying about, storing, purchasing, and desiring more possessions. Perhaps there are small steps you might take in this practice of renunciation and simplicity. How many pairs of shoes is enough? Will that new set of golf clubs really change your game? In what part of the culture of consumption do you no longer wish to participate? What would it be like to use the objects you already own until they truly were worn out? Perhaps you might begin by fasting from buying anything on the Sabbath. Notice the pull to purchase or to have more and decide that you wish to be free simply to be in the presence of the Holy.

Leaning in further, giving away financial resources, and allowing God to direct what we do with our resources are even deeper opportunities for spiritual growth. The biblical tradition is to give one tenth of one's income as an offering to God. Deuteronomy gives instructions that the first fruits of the ground are to be offered. When you consider how hungry our ancestors must have been in that fragile time as the last bits of the previous year's stored harvest ran out, the offering of first fruits must have been very dear. Accompanying that offering is a recitation of remembrance that we were once a people enslaved who by the grace of God alone are now set free (Deuteronomy 26:1-10). The giving of an offering is a powerful act of trust. It is an unclenching of the grasping hand that so often clings to things that only seem life giving but in fact are entrapments. When we give away the resources that we hold dear, we are restating a profound trust in God's provision for us and opening a door into a holy contentment.

> The apostle Paul gave us a glimpse of that life-grounding trust when he wrote, "I have learned to be content with whatever I have. I know what it is to have little, and I know what it is to have plenty. In any

and all circumstances I have learned the secret of being well-fed and of going hungry, of having plenty and of being in need. I can do all things through God who strengthens me." (Philippians 4:11-13)

The offering of a tithe can lead us into joyful adventures of trusting God. I can recall a season of what felt like miracles when my husband and I were starting out as young pastors in Texas. We had committed to giving a tithe, though it truly felt like a stretch and a financially foolish move. In short order, a series of what must certainly be first world problems came upon us. The electricity on the house was found to be not up to code and would cost thousands to repair and, in the span of a week, first one car was wrecked hitting a deer, and the other crushed in an accident. We were sorely tempted to hold back our tithes to the church seemingly out of necessity. Surely God would understand we needed this money to fix our house and the cars. But then an even more enticing and exciting idea arose from prayer. God has asked us to truly trust and to offer our tithe in confidence of God's provision. The grace moment happened for us when, instead of panicking about these bills, God gave us a posture of curiosity. "Okay, Lord," we prayed, "we cannot wait to see how you are going to surprise us by sorting this out." It was a prayer of timid confidence.

I shared our situation with a few trusted friends at church and asked them to join me in prayer. We did not know until then that we were blessed with a friend who owned a construction company that did home wiring and who offered to repair our wiring free of charge. Another friend said the Lord had put it on her heart to get one of our cars up and running and she wanted to do it as a gift to the Lord. The tears in my eyes that day were both for joy and astonished gratitude at God's generosity and my friend's faithfulness. There was more than enough to go around. By allowing a financial gap that I knew I could not fill, I was blessed to be able to see God in action meeting our needs. That is not to say we were testing God; we didn't need God to prove anything. Our experience was one of trying to live faithfully and being joyfully surprised at the way in which God met our need. The experience led me to understand that if we are always playing it safe, we may not be leaving room enough for God to show God's astonishing love and provision for us.

One group of people who live these biblical principles of generosity and financial integrity in a profound way is the Iona Community. The Iona community was founded on the Scottish island of Iona in 1938 by pastor George MacCleod in the context of the great depression.

MacCleod took unemployed skilled craftsmen and young clergymen to the island to rebuild the monastic quarters of the Abbey and to rediscover the power of living in community. What began in that time has grown to a worldwide ecumenical dispersed community of faithful who subscribe to a rule of life that includes daily prayer and Bible reading, action for justice and peace, planning and accounting for the use of time, meeting with and being accountable to others, and sharing and accounting for the use of personal resources including money. While most people would be deeply uncomfortable even hinting about their income level to other people, members of the Iona community disclose it fully to one another and then meet to discuss what is actually necessary for each person's situation and what is disposable for the good of the community. Once the amount of disposable income is identified, a formula for distribution is used to share these funds with the community, purposes decided by each family group, and a travel fund. Members are also asked to account for their use of the earth's natural resources.

While this community's accountability might seem far too personal for some, for others it is exactly the kind of incentive needed to live a life fully available for God. How we spend our money and our time truly does reveal our priorities. If our desire is to make life in God a central part of our lives, then that choice must be reflected in how we spend both our time and what we do with our resources. It might seem paralyzing to choose among the many agencies that serve the needs of the world. There are many wonderful and trustworthy groups to support. You may or may not be part of a local congregation, but you can still share some of the material blessing you have with your community and the world. A great place to start is with what you love. Often God uses these emotions to draw us into relationship for service. Are you passionate about children? Find an agency that is doing good work with kids in your community and volunteer with them and fund their work. It is also possible that you might be called to sponsor a child on the other side of the globe. What we spend each week on takeout food or coffee could provide clean water, books, and health care for a month in a developing country. Do you ache every time you see someone holding a cardboard sign on the side of the road asking for help? Find the agency in your community that is working to solve the homeless problem and make a monthly contribution. One family I know puts together backpacks with nonperishable food, coupons for a local diner, clean socks, and toiletries for such occasions. They also make sure to include a note sharing a prayer for the recipient. Do you wish women were better treated in the world? Choose an agency that is working to promote self-sufficiency and economic independence for women. Throughout scripture God calls us to care for the widows and orphans, meaning the most vulnerable in the world. Each one of us, no matter how poor, can contribute to the wellbeing of others. Doing so is an act that declares our freedom from the tyranny of myth that there is not enough to go around. Reaching out with God's love and unclenching our fists to share with others is a healing act for all involved and a practice which blesses not only those who receive, but also those who give.

SAMPLE EXERCISES

A guided meditation based on Mark 10:17-22

Begin by finding a quiet place where you will not be disturbed and allow yourself at least a half an hour for this exercise. Imagine that you are in the time and place where Jesus has been teaching and healing people and you have a longing to learn from him. He has just invited the gathered crowd to become like children, innocent, vulnerable, and trusting in their relationship with God. You are aware that you want more of this life of which he speaks. You ask Jesus how to have more of this abundant life, and he answers that you are to honor God in all that you do and say. You have tried to do this, and you share with him those ways. He looks at you with deep love. He wants the very best for you. Jesus wants you to be free from all that encumbers you so that God can have a primary place in your life. He tells you there is one more thing you must do, "Go and sell your possessions and give the money to the poor." He assures you that you will have treasure in heaven, and then you will be able to come and follow him.

Write down the questions and concerns that come to mind with this invitation, and listen and write what Jesus offers in response.

Hang up your watch

One of the most powerful first steps in reclaiming a more natural sense of the rhythm of time, especially when we are trying to turn our attention to God, can be getting away from our time pieces. A group of friends I know try to spend one weekend every couple months together savoring one another's company and the presence of the Holy. They begin the weekend with a ritual of taking off their watches and hanging them on the chandelier. It is an act of liberation and defiance of being ruled by a schedule. They eat when they are hungry, they sleep until they wake up. They listen for the promptings of the Spirit and often at sunset they gather to celebrate the blessings of the day. Consider choosing a day to live without your watch. Instead of asking what time it is, ask the Spirit to lead you through the day. Allow yourself to rest when you feel sleepy and to eat when you are hungry. Resist other technology on this day and see if you can simply allow yourself to enjoy the flow of the day in relative quiet. Don't set goals about what you will and will not do. Trust God to suggest the next right movement. Perhaps you will be led on a walk or into a conversation with an old friend. Maybe a book will fall in your lap and you will be blessed. As the sun sets on this day, take time to journal about what you noticed, both the things that were challenging and delightful.

Observing the Hours of Prayer

In a later chapter on prayer we will learn about the set times and ancient rhythm of prayer throughout the day. Review that section and see if you feel called to come into relationship with time in a new way using the tools outlined there.

A Careful Accounting

For this practice, you might consider inviting a trusted friend who shares your values and commitment to God to work with you. It is possible to do your finances by yourself, but there is something very powerful about presenting your financial situation to another on behalf of God. Begin by giving thanks to God for all that you have been given and express your desire to place all these resources at God's disposal. Next, write your income at the top of a page of paper and then take a careful look at all the necessary expenses in your life; housing, food, health care, and basic needs like clothing and utilities. Who is dependent on you for their care? Include these in the tally of necessary expenses. When you have deducted the truly necessary expenses from your income, you now have the amount of your disposable income. To whom or to what purpose is God inviting you to dedicate a portion of this money? How might you bless others with what you have been given?

Conscious Consuming and Exploring the Concept of Fair Trade

The American culture and economy is based largely on consumerism. We go shopping as a form of recreation and entertainment. In contrast, this practice invites us to become conscious of the ways in which we are using the resources God has entrusted to us and to consider if we are using them to the best purpose. To begin you might choose a period of time for observation, perhaps two weeks. You might begin by mapping out all the planned purchases you anticipate. From coffee to new clothes—is each of those purchases necessary? Are any of those a duplication of something you already own in abundance or might borrow from a neighbor? This is not about cutting back on spending necessarily, though that may be an added benefit. This is about becoming actively conscious of where your money goes, who it is supporting, and considering alternate uses for those funds. As you look at your anticipated purchases, do you know the conditions in which your items were produced or brought to market? How might you go about researching that? Do the producers of those items get a living wage for what they are producing? Consider looking into Fair Trade certified items. A quick web search for fair trade items can offer up an abundance of options from coffee to clothes in which the producers are guaranteed a fair wage for the items they are selling and your purchase can benefit an individual artisan or farming community. While Fair Trade does have its challenges and limitations, much like the certification of organic foods, it is still a concept worth exploring as we consider whom we wish to support with our market purchases.

FOR FURTHER READING

Dana, Maryann McKibben. *Sabbath in the Suburbs*. St. Louis: Chalice, 2012.
Dawn, Marva. *Keeping the Sabbath Wholly*. Grand Rapids: Eerdmans, 1989.
Escamilla, Paul. *Longing for Enough in a Culture of More*. Nashville: Abingdon, 2007.
Foster, Richard. *Freedom of Simplicity*. New York: HarperCollins, 1981.
Heschel, Abraham Joshua. *The Sabbath*. New York: HarperCollins, 1951.
Honoré, Carl. *In Praise of Slowness: Challenging the Cult of Speed*. New York: HarperCollins, 2004.
Muller, Wayne. *Sabbath: Restoring The Sacred Rhythm of Rest*. New York: Bantam, 1999.
Postema, Don. *Catch your Breath: God's Invitation to Sabbath Rest*. Grand Rapids: CRC, 1997.

Chapter 5

Praying: The Practice of Companionship with God

*I remember my grandmother's prayer. Every day she would go to
her room and sit in her rocking chair. The door was open, so no one
was closed out, but we understood she was not to be interrupted.
She sat in that chair, rocking, for up to an hour. Mostly she was silent.
But every so often, she would sigh, "Oh, God." That was all she
ever said, but she usually said it more than once, in a different tone
of voice each time. When she came back out, she was just as usual,
except for a quality of radiance about her. How I longed to do
whatever it was she did there!*

Fellowship in Prayer, Author unknown[1]

Companionship with Mystery

Prayer is the primary means of our relationship with the Holy. While
prayer is about words, it is more truly about a whole way of personal and communal presence to daily life. Initially a conversation,
prayer increasingly becomes a rhythm of heart and mind that finds
the Beloved in all things. As Esther de Waal observes, a "life lived in
God's presence is a growing, permeating consciousness of what that
presence means."[2] I write as a person formed in the Benedictine spirit,
meaning that I am learning to seek God within life experience. *Lectio
divina*[3] teaches me to look further than first impressions, and to attend
to every aspect of creation with deepening levels of awareness for the

graces revealed within. Just as a painting embodies the "hand" of the artist, so the created world embodies the mark of the Creator. The book of Job reflects this wisdom: "ask the animals, the birds, the plants, and the fish . . . and they will teach you. . . . In God's hand is the life of every living thing and the breath of every human being" (Job 12:7-10). The life of prayer brings growing awareness of the pervasive presence of the Holy in every place and time.

The reality that God is eternal Mystery means that we humans will never be able to describe, contain, or master the Holy. Yet those with a spiritual longing can make a twofold affirmation: (1) the world is God's—God is somehow present within our experienced material world; and (2) I am God's—in some unimaginable way, the Mystery that is God reaches out to me and claims me. A persistent element of the Mystery is the ongoing human hunch that God is "in *personal* relationship with embodied possibilities."[4] However we think of God, we are haunted by the sense that we are not alone. God is not confined by time and space, but the perennial human intuition is that God is *present* in time and space. Humans may speak of the "otherness" that surrounds us as the world of Ideals (Plato), the Atman (Hinduism), the inner life, Jehovah, or the Trinity. But whatever the term, the referent is Mystery. The desire is for connection, for companionship.

But how? How do humans find companionship with something always Other? The issue is compounded by the historical idea, especially associated with the scientific revolution, that the Mystery of God is merely like the "mystery" in murder mystery novels, that is, something that can and will eventually be "solved" and mastered by human ingenuity. No longer did humans need the "crutch" of belief in something beyond our knowing, because we could "know" everything! A great deal of ink has been spilled on this idea of human mastery, but it seems not to have significantly touched the inevitable human longing for the More. Religious doctrine and ritual may not have the claim on human hearts that they once had (in the United States in particular), but still a vast majority of people describe themselves as "spiritual."

Cynthia Bourgeault offers a useful way to discuss companionship with the Holy, honoring both the claims of science and those of the spirit, as she describes the intelligence of the human mind as integrated with the intelligence of the "moving center" and the intelligence of the "emotional center." We well know the gifts of the intellectual center for reasoning, discriminating, analyzing; but perhaps we don't recognize that these are primarily gifts of separating and denying. They are valuable gifts, but not well suited to spiritual work. "Trying to find faith with the intellectual center is something like trying to play a violin with a saw: it's simply the wrong tool for the job."[5]

In contrast, the gifts of the other two centers are our strong arms in spiritual practice. The moving center includes both the instinctive center, regulating the inner operational systems of the body; and the moving center proper, operating our outward and voluntary interactions with the physical world, the five senses, movement, and rhythm. Repetition can connect us with the steady pulsations of breath, heartbeat and instinct. Certain gestures strengthen interior rhythms of balance, relaxation, making contact, and embracing. The moving center can be seen as an affirming force, connecting us with parts of ourselves unreachable solely by the mind.

And the emotional, or heart center, has long been understood in spiritual practice as the human organ best suited to reach for God. While recognizing that emotions can be misdirected or out of control, the early Christian theologians saw God as loving and beautiful, desirable to the human heart, and creating within us the emotional passions. Thus, they conclude that the powerful sense of yearning for something unseen and unknowable comes from the human heart *in response to* the invitation of the infinitely good. The heart "is our antenna, so to speak, given to us to orient us toward the divine radiance and to synchronize our being with its more subtle movements."[6] Even Augustine of Hippo, often associated with a core conviction about human sinfulness, observes, "The entire life of a good Christian is in fact an exercise of holy desire. You do not yet see what you long for, but the very act of desiring prepares you."[7]

The whole human being is involved in our relationship with God, and when we consider other human centers of wisdom alongside the rational, we see why we humans are so persistent in our desire for a "spiritual life." It seems our DNA is encoded with the awareness of both the material and spiritual worlds we inhabit. The goal of practice—especially the practice of prayer—is to integrate those worlds.

Pause to reflect:
- *As you begin to ponder the practice of prayer, what is at the heart of your desire? You might consider reading Psalm 42 to reflect on this question. How have you known deep longing for the presence of God in your own life?*
- *Reflect on the centers described above. From which center: intellectual, moving, or emotional, do you most reach out for God?*

Beginning to Pray

"Help me." This is perhaps the most common prayer, and a foundational one. Until we realize that we need help, for whatever reason, we are not ready for prayer. But once we know we need help, we need to know someone is listening. So the next prayer is "hear me." We could probably pray the whole psalter with those two words, and one other, "Thanks!"[8]

Simply put, prayer is the practice of conversation with God, some talking, some listening, some silent reflection. Sometimes people ask, "How do I pray?" There is no simple formula, and no "right" way. Begin. Start where you are. Stop and listen. Pray as you can, not as you can't. On the whole, God doesn't "answer" loudly or quickly. Settle in. Recollect the stages in beginning any relationship, a little tentative and uncertain. Consider the importance of mutual trust and regard, and the fact that even someone deeply loved can surprise us. Remember that the simple *desire* to pray is a gift from God, and God wants to help.

At various times in life, our prayer changes. Perhaps a practice of prayer we've had for a long time seems to dry up. Perhaps a crisis in our lives takes over for a time, and we don't feel we can pray at all. A type of prayer that works well for another person may not suit us. A friend of mine once complained that much of prayer practice was taught by introverts, and she was too much of an extrovert to get with it! So it is well to be acquainted with many possibilities, knowing that if one or another form of prayer doesn't touch us at the moment, there are multiple ways to deepen our communication with God.

The Rich Resources of Christian Tradition

Christianity is an historical religion, emphasizing the incarnation—Jesus born of woman, fully human. We are predisposed to look for God within time, welcoming images and actual life experiences as God-blessed ways of communication, in a form of prayer called *kataphatic* (with images). Our tradition gives important places to memory, imagination, and the body in prayer. Memory is highlighted in recollection of the saving acts of God in history at the Red Sea and in Christ's holy meal of the Eucharist. Imagination is welcomed in the scripture's constant use of metaphor and parable. The body is central as we sit and stand and kneel in worship, sing enthusiastically, and physically come forward to receive the sacramental bread and wine. Many Christian prayer forms use images and words and life experience as ways to receive and welcome God in our lives. And, not surprisingly, our primary "measure" of good prayer is growth in compassion, evidence that our prayer actually influences and enriches the way we live each day. The classic Christian spiritual "test" of a spiritual person is: "The fruit of the Spirit is love, joy, peace, patience, kindness, generosity, faithfulness, gentleness, and self-control" (Galatians 5:22).

Discursive Prayer

The most frequent elements in spoken prayers are overlapping, but also somewhat discrete. These five elements are:

- **Thanksgiving**: living life in appreciation for what God is doing for us, and expressing that gratitude;
- **Intercession**: praying for others;
- **Confession:** admitting our sins and asking to be forgiven;
- **Petition:** praying for our own needs, and that our lives may be more and more in harmony with God's will for us; and
- **Adoration**: looking at God, loving God, praising God, and abandoning ourselves to God in gladness.

All five of these elements are central to a full life of prayer.

Thanksgiving

Prayer is framed in thanksgiving, beginning and end. One might even say that the measure of a relationship with God is a life filled with thanksgiving. I recall a time when this came home to me clearly. I had worked in public service for some time, during which period I didn't go to church and didn't consciously think much about God. In a sense, I believe I had submerged a relationship with God into what I felt was service to God's people. I was successful outwardly, but increasingly restless inwardly. Deciding to leave that work and attending to my restlessness, I enrolled in seminary. Later when I returned to visit some friends from the earlier period, I realized that I puzzled them—not, I think, by any overt expression of evangelism, but simply because my language was so full of gratitude! Previously I felt that I *deserved* all that I worked so hard to achieve, but now I knew that I could never accomplish for myself those things which most satisfied my deep longing for abundant life.

Thanksgiving is a way of opening ourselves to God. If there is no thanksgiving in me, it is impossible to know myself as gifted. But as I begin to express thanksgiving, more and more room opens in me for God's joyful gifts.

> **Pause to reflect:** *A good way to work with the prayer of thanks-giving is to settle into a quiet time and place, and take a few minutes to write down things for which you are thankful. Start with something, anything. Keep adding. Keep writing. Keep reflecting. After a while, stop and look over your list, and select the five most important items for which you are thankful right now. If you are working with a part-ner, share those five items each with the other. Finally, take one of the five items to keep as your "mantra" for the next week, something to hold in your heart or under your nose like a flower to which you periodically return. Deepen your gratitude for that particular thing. Notice what effect, if any, this prayer has in you.*[9]

Intercession

Intercession is prayer for others, and it probably forms the bulk of our prayer. Certainly it is the easiest prayer to do "in public," and possibly the one that makes us feel best about ourselves for carrying concern in our hearts for others in need. [But beware of pride: I've often prayed over a meal for the needs of others, but I was caught up short once when someone prayed for the needs *and the gifts* of others.] Even so, there are many questions about intercessory prayer: exactly what to pray for, how it really "works," how to decide what to pray for in a world of so much hurt, and so forth. I recommend C. S. Lewis's *Letters to Malcolm* as a thoughtful and straightforward discussion of some of these questions.[10]

One insight I cherish about praying for others comes from the Peace Pilgrim:

> *If a person returns to my mind for prayer. . . . I reach out—my divine nature reaches out—to contact their divine nature. Then I have the feeling of lifting them, lifting them, lifting them, and I have the feeling of bringing God's light to them. I try to envision them bathed in God's light, and finally I do see them standing and reaching out their arms bathed in golden light. At that point I leave them in God's hands.*[11]

Not everyone can visualize in this way, but even without being able to "see" an image, it seems wise to mentally bring someone to God and leave them in God's hands (in addition to any practical help we can offer).

The prayer of intercession is, of course, not just relevant for private prayer, but also for public common prayer. Every Sunday in my church we offer one of six forms of "Prayers of the People" from the Book of Common Prayer.[12] Yet even those of us familiar with the BCP may not notice that all six forms follow a common format of elements important for us to consider as a community of faith. This format considers in turn:

- The universal church (and I add: and all people of faith)
- The nation and those in authority
- The welfare of the world
- Concerns of the local community
- Those who suffer or are in trouble, and those who care for them
- Those who are departed (and I add: and those newly born)

I like to "festoon" this outline, supplementing each broad category with the present concerns that are uppermost in my mind, and I often do this with a group as well. This format above is not necessarily comprehensive but is rather a solid foundation from which to build personal and communal intercessions, beyond those nearest and dearest expanding to others in our communities and across the earth.

The world today offers a bewildering array of potential concerns for which to pray, and the daily dose of news can numb us to give up even trying to offer prayers for others. The way I try to think about my intercessory ministry is to consider this question: "What brokenness in the world breaks my heart?" And although many issues cry out to me, I find that a few regularly enter my heart and mind for intercessory prayer. Although some of these change over time, this question does help me focus my call to intercessory ministry.

Confession

To consider confession, we must begin with reflection on how our life is falling short of what we hope for it, and how we are responsible for—or contribute to—that falling short. Private confession is generally no longer required for Christians, but there may be times—when we feel especially burdened, during the period of Lent, annually as a "clearinghouse"—one may profitably choose to do so. It is well to prepare in a "soul-searching" time, referred to by twelve-step organizations as "a fearless moral inventory."

Some "sins" involve our active or passive participation in problems embodied in the existing social structure. The Ash Wednesday Litany in the BCP reviews some of these: our blindness to human need and suffering, our indifference to injustice and cruelty, the waste and pollution of God's creation.[13] A "four-fold blessing" I recently received struck my heart as a useful set of questions to help me see and confess my participation in structural sins of our society:

- *God give me a restless discomfort about easy answers, half-truths and superficial relationships;*
- *God grant me holy anger at injustice, oppression, and exploitation of people;*
- *God give me the gift of tears to shed with those who suffer from pain, rejection, starvation, or the loss of all that they cherish; and*
- *God grant me enough foolishness to believe that I really CAN make a difference in this world.*[14]

Turning to personal sins, we may wish to prepare for confession by reviewing standard lists of "sins," such as the Ten Commandments, the Beatitudes, or the Baptismal Covenant, but for the most part, if we are already trying to live a spiritual life, those lists may not be of much value. I recommend turning to our own experience, and asking ourselves "What questions is my life raising?" There may be an obvious and present issue, causing us to feel a special current burden that is leading us into this preparation for confession. In all, ask the Holy Spirit to show you the root difficulty, enabling you to see beyond sin to the cause of it in habits of mind or action; and to see beyond your sin to its cure, the abundant grace of God in Christ.

Having prepared, it is wise to share your inventory with someone you trust to receive it respectfully, though it need not be an ordained person. However, one of the central aspects of confession is the receiving of absolution and restoration to full communion with God and the community. So, after you have confessed, ask the other to say some words to you that will assist you to receive the awareness of reconciliation that is a deep source of joy.

Petition

Inevitably confession leads us to awareness of our fundamental limitations. We may say with Paul, "I do not understand my own actions. I do not do what I want, but I do the very thing I hate" (Romans 7:15). A seminary professor once revealed that he did not expect confession to be a matter of (Baskin-Robbins) 31 flavors of ice cream! He encouraged us not to work to come up with something new to confess each time, but simply and honestly to bring ourselves, as we are, as God knows us to be, with our inherent limitations. We do repent, but above all, we realize we must rely on God's help.

The point of petition is to know we need help, and to ask God for what we need. A deep longing of our heart is for union with God, yet we cannot quite "do it" ourselves. Petition offers a wonderful opportunity to ask God's help in moving toward deeper, truer levels of ourselves in relation to God. Recall the words mentioned in chapter 1 of the twelfth century monk who assures us that "God does not wait until the longing soul has said all its say, but breaks in upon the middle of its prayer, running to meet it in all haste."[15]

The first question Jesus asks in John's Gospel is one we are invited to reflect upon more and more deeply throughout our lives: "What do you want?" (John 1:39). Why should Jesus (God) ask what we want? Unless and until we know what we need and can ask for it, God respectfully restrains response. When I was first married, I used to get upset with my husband for not *knowing* what I wanted. It's not quite the same situation with God, I realize, but I did learn in my marriage that it was unfair of me *not to ask* for what I desired. And then I realized that one of the main reasons I didn't ask was because I didn't want to be refused. Genuinely to offer myself in vulnerability to another with a real request (rather than a demand) puts me at that other's mercy. What if he said no? And yet how dishonest of me to wait unspoken in hope, or worse yet, to try to gain my objective by manipulation.

Perhaps we have been told that it is selfish to ask for ourselves, but I think it is essential. Genuine vulnerability to another is necessary for authentic relationship. Most of the time, as persons and communities, we surround ourselves with defensive walls to make sure that others do not know nor take advantage of our fears or weaknesses. Of course it makes sense to be cautious and discerning, but consider how much we lose by not allowing ourselves to be genuinely engaged with another, mutually reinforcing and maturing. It is a commonplace that the risk of deeply loving necessarily includes the pain of losing another to death. Shall we for that reason resist love? Loving takes courage, and loving God no less courage. The practice of companionship with God will take all we can give—and return it manifold, but the risk must come first.

The Psalms reassure us that any way we ask or pray to God is okay. The range of emotions offered in the Psalms is almost shocking to modern ears—anger, bitterness, self-justification, as well as love and longing, delight and praise. When we pray, we may have no sense of answering response for a time, or we may sense a negative response. What we can count on is continued companionship, continuing love.

Adoration

Is adoration different from thanksgiving? Yes, although in practice we do not often make the distinction. Thanksgiving is appreciation for God's gifts, whereas adoration is loving God for God's sake, rather than for anything God has done or is doing for us. Bernard of Clairvaux observes that in prayer, we tend to progress from (1) loving ourselves for our own sake, (2) to loving God for our own sake, (3) to loving God for God's sake, (4) to loving ourselves for God's sake, being entirely transfused into the will of God.[16] *Adoration is being wholly centered in the divine glory and majesty, not giving thanks for gifts to ourselves or others, but simply rejoicing in the Giver.* I imagine how God might respond first to the prayer, "O Lord, I am a worm!" and second to the prayer, "O God, how wonderful you are!" Of course, over time we may pray both, and in God's kindness, God receives in love whatever prayer we offer, but I long to be a person who can wholeheartedly pray "O God, how wonderful you are!"

Many of the Christian canticles are songs of adoration, for example the beginning of Mary of Nazareth's song of praise, "My soul proclaims the greatness of the Lord, my spirit rejoices in God my Savior" or the *Te Deum*, "You are God: we praise you." Psalms 104 and 145 are wonderful to pray with in adoration: "Bless the Lord, O my soul; O Lord my God, how excellent is your greatness!" and "I will exalt you, O God and bless your Name forever." What a mystery it is that we are invited to bless God! Yet how else can we understand early morning birdsong or twilight sunset at the ocean, except as adoration of God?!

Other Traditional Christian Prayer Practices

Other important prayer practices of the Christian tradition include (1) prayer without ceasing, (2) walking meditation (3) praying the hours of the day, (4) praying with nature, and (5) meditation/contemplation.

Prayer without Ceasing

Prayer need not be complicated. Given that the goal is to become increasingly alive to the holy presence among us, a simple formula, repeated continuously, can be a helpful way to move our awareness of God from a mental thing to something that joins the rhythm of our heart and lungs to become a subtle but constant presence within us. Two "formula prayers" have been used for centuries to this purpose.

- One of them is rooted in Psalm 70, verse 2: *"O God, come to my assistance; O Lord make haste to help me."*
- The other is taken from the plea of blind Bartimaeus to Jesus in Mark's gospel (10:46-52): *"Jesus, son of David, have mercy on me."*

The latter phrase has been developed into an expansive form of prayer, initially presented as a story in *The Way of the Pilgrim*, and later taught in detail in the *Philokalia*.[17] It is considered an extraordinarily useful way to "pray without ceasing."[18] I find one or other of these forms especially helpful in times when I am fearful or anxious, as the prayer reminds me of God's presence and grounds me.

Walking Meditation

I often practice formula prayer while walking, first attending to the rhythm of my pace, then to the rhythm of breath and heartbeat, and gradually adding the prayer rhythm until I can sense the prayer moving down into my heart. The old monastic cloisters were built between the church and the residential areas, and the monastics would walk around the cloister praying one of these prayers or a prayer antiphon which stayed in their mind and soul.

Another ancient, and now well known walking prayer, is walking the labyrinth. A labyrinth is not a maze (one cannot get lost in it, for it is a singular route in and out), but it does wind around and around from "outside" to an inner center, where one may sit for a time, and then walk back to the beginning. The most famous Christian labyrinth is on the floor of Chartres Cathedral, and today many canvas labyrinths are available for use in local communities. Walking the labyrinth, one pays attention to the thoughts that arise, exploring the many dimensions of their life experience at present in relationship to images the labyrinth brings to mind, and especially in the center space, bringing everything to be offered to God. Books and pilgrimages by and with Episcopal priest, Lauren Artress, are excellent guides.[19]

Praying the Hours of the Day

The world is God's and I am God's. This fundamental Christian affirmation rescues us from thinking all is lost and/or that everything depends upon our being where we are and doing what we do. We are not alone, not abandoned to our own (limited) resources. But we forget. For most of us, it requires only a few hours (or minutes) to take everything back into our own hands. The prayer of the hours of the day is intended to remedy or at least limit our forgetfulness.

One of the Hebrew psalms calls to God, "Seven times a day do I praise you!" (Psalm 119:164), and Benedict's sixth century guidance for prayer in his *Rule* picks up this phrase in specifying that the monastic day should be punctuated with Lauds (daybreak), Prime (immediately following, at the "first hour" of the Roman day), Terce (9 am), Sext (noon), None (3pm), Vespers (dusk), and Compline (bedtime). Benedict also added an early morning Vigils office (watching for the dawn, approximately 2 am) which is an office of readings.[20] The prayer of these hours (called the *Opus Dei*, or the Work of God) gradually spread through most of the Christian monastic communities in the West and later in the world, as well as many of the cathedral communities. It is intended to be a prayer of the community, and is fundamentally a prayer of remembering that this is God's world.

Most of the prayer times are brief, containing the chanting of several psalms, brief readings from scripture, and the Lord's Prayer, although it is possible today to get books of elaborate prayer "offices," each of which can take some time. When Thomas Cranmer in sixteenth century England wrote the Anglican Book of Common Prayer, he condensed the eight hours of prayer into two major ones, morning prayer and evening prayer, and included a brief office of compline that follows Benedict's outline closely. The point is simply that since the early Hebrew period, not only monks and nuns, but people of Jewish and Christian faiths have had some sort of practice of praying regularly throughout the day.

As I have studied these times of the prayer hours, I realized that although they are spaced about evenly throughout the hours of the day, they are also carefully linked in history to significant events of faith, corresponding to what might be natural human emotions during a normal day.[21]

Praying with Nature

In some periods of Christianity, nature was considered to be "suspect," a source of potential delights and temptations that might draw the mind away from God. Thankfully, that attitude has mostly disappeared, for how could it be consistent with Jesus's ever-present awareness of the marvelous beauty of bird feathers, the astonishing growth of tiny seeds, the marvelous gift of water for thirst? God is not confined in nature (a view called pantheism) but is revealed in nature (called panentheism). As I trust will be obvious from this chapter, creation is marked by the wondrous creative hand of the One who created all, and thus can be a powerful sign of the Mystery's presence among us. It is not really necessary to offer any special techniques for praying with nature, if one appreciates Abraham Heschel's definition of Sabbath as ceasing the work of creating (things) to marvel at the gift of creation.[22] Helpful specifies are offered in the previous chapter (4).

Meditation/Contemplation

Both Western and Eastern spiritual traditions include meditation and contemplation. It is somewhat confusing that the terms are used one way in the East, and the opposite way in the West. In the West, meditation tends to mean discursive thought, while contemplation refers to an imageless, wordless resting in God (called *apophatic* prayer). In the East, contemplation means discursive thought and meditation means a self-emptying presence to the Holy. In the following paragraphs, we'll use the typical Western definitions.

Both traditions honor both meditative and contemplative modes of prayer, and consider them to be linked. When people are invited into a time of imageless, wordless prayer, generally speaking they are offered "tokens" enabling the mind to remain steady. An Eastern metaphor describes riding an elephant through a village; if the elephant has nothing in his trunk as he goes past various stalls of foods, he will be likely to pluck up a banana here, a melon there. Needless to say, the stall owners are not happy about it, so the mahouts have learned the importance of giving the elephant a stick to hold in his trunk before they enter a village. With the trunk absorbed in the job of holding the stick, mischief is much less likely.

In Western tradition, Teresa of Avila uses a different metaphor of a monkey in the attic. Both images are meant to suggest the tendency of the mind to wander into all sorts of irrelevant things if it is "empty-handed," so to speak. Thus, a number of tools have been used over time to help the mind settle, while the heart focuses on God below conscious awareness. Fortunately, these tools are readily available and can serve a variety of preferences. One of the most common is to begin a time of contemplation with a focus on the breath, allowing oneself to slow down with each breath, moving deeper and deeper into quiet, and allowing a slow, steady breath to hold the mind quiet for a time. Another common tool is a mantra or a special prayer word(s), such as "Jesus, mercy," "Love," or "Hear my prayer." Repetition of the mantra is used in the beginning until inner quiet comes upon us, then released until inner noise comes back, then gently repeated again, and so forth throughout the prayer time. A candle may be used, or an icon, quiet music in the background, the soft chanting of an antiphon. Each of these tools allows a focus on something sensory which gradually leads the mind into quiet, and which can readily move the mind back into silence as needed.

Contemplative prayer practice is widely in use today, and there are many excellent sources of information on this practice. Abbot Thomas Keating is one of the originating contemporary teachers of this method and the chapter on Gratitude includes more about this practice.[23]

The Gift of Hope

Why do we pray? As one of the primary means of our companionship with God, prayer helps us learn to hear and recognize God's communication with us. Moving deeper into this companionship, and noticing more frequently God's presence to and with us, we learn to trust the Mysterious Presence with our lives. We have less need to control and manage everything around us, as it becomes clearer to us that in fact, we are not in control anyway. Even when we think we are brilliantly capable, things often go awry. Consider the unintended and often harmful consequences of technological advances, or the troubles faced by our loved ones, no matter how carefully we try to protect them.

Today's world is full of problems, many of which fill our souls with grief. Some of those problems we bring on ourselves, some come upon us willy-nilly. How are we to face these situations? We can try to deny their seriousness. We can let ourselves sink into discouragement and despair. But real prayer gives us a more positive option. We recall ourselves to the basic fact that the world is God's and we are God's—not just those of us who are Christians or avowed persons of faith or intentionally spiritual—we all are God's and living in God's world.

What can that mean, if God doesn't definitively intervene to stop all this trouble? What does trust in God mean, if bad things happen to good people? No sacred text of which I am aware promises that we will never have trouble. The Mystery that we call God is truly beyond our knowing, and ultimately we cannot wrap our small minds around God's purposes, but what the faithful practice of prayer can teach us is that we are companioned, we are befriended, we will never be alone. We can look back on the stories of our faith traditions, and on our personal stories, and see the times when things looked very bad, yet God found a way to bring goodness out of our very worst moments. Oh yes, there exist violence, loss, misunderstanding, and frightful strangers in our world, but prayer can bring us hope: hope for things unseen and unimagined, yet hope nonetheless even and especially in times like these.

SAMPLE EXERCISES

Praying with Words

Look back to the five elements of discursive prayer: Thanksgiving, Intercession, Confession, Petition, and Adoration. Choose one on which to focus and begin your practice of prayer. You may use the sections above to direct your prayer, or follow a pattern of your own choosing.

Self-Awareness

In a quiet and relaxed time, let your breathing settle you. Give yourself time to enter deeply into your most authentic self-awareness and ask yourself three questions (below). When you have adequate answers for today, put your knowledge in the form of one or more petitions to God. Sit in silence and listen. Observe what, if anything, happens today or within the next week or two.

- What are my hopes and dreams, my deep longings?
- What do I lack, where do I hurt, what seems consistently to block my hopes?
- What am I willing to give up or let go, in order to receive what I desire?

Body Prayer

Sometimes it is helpful to express adoration and praise of God through the body. One may practice prayer with upraised arms and dancing, or through the voice upraised in song. One might try "interpreting" one of the psalms of praise in body language, or paraphrasing it in one's own words, to deepen one's expression of joyful adoration.

Praying the Hours

If it is desirable to try praying these hours for a time, consider taking only five to ten minutes per period, focusing on one attitude and reminding oneself of God's continuing care in each period.

- Before fully waking: Take a moment to be radically expectant for God in today's activities;
- At or after breakfast: Praise God and rejoice in the wonder of God's being;
- As you begin the workday: Dedicate yourself to be God's co-worker in all the day brings;
- Mid-morning: Seek God's strength to act as you would throughout the day;
- Noontime: (traditionally noon and midnight are considered to be the moments when we are furthest from God, most at risk in spiritual conflict, whereas the "hinges" of 6am and 6pm are believed to be the times most likely to sense oneself close to God's presence, hence:) Acknowledge that life is difficult, with many pulls and pushes in all directions, and simply be where you are at this moment;
- Mid-afternoon: Persevere in faith;
- At (before/after) dinner-time: Give thanks for the day and its fullness; and
- Bedtime: Acknowledge your need for God's care and rest.

As you pray on these occasions, be aware that you are joining a large group of people, scattered over all the earth, in all times zones, who are joining you in lifting their thoughts to God in this way.

Praying with Nature

First, let yourself be drawn to an object in nature, and if it is convenient, settle yourself comfortably with the thing in hand (a leaf, a pebble, a nut, a feather, whatever). Get acquainted with your natural object with all your senses: how does it smell and feel, what is its weight, texture and temperature, and so forth. What is it like? What does it do? Discover all you can, being very gentle and reverent in your attention.

Then identify imaginatively with the natural object and "become" it. If you were this object, what would your history be? What would your chief gifts and limitations be? Where did you come from, and where are you going? As a little part of nature, what is important to you? What is your existence like? Describe yourself as this creation. Say to yourself silently, "I am. . . ." Finally your object may have some wisdom specifically for you. Ask for this, and then listen quietly to whatever comes to mind. Don't hurry and be respectful. If a prayer forms in you, express it in whatever way seems right.

FOR FURTHER READING

Artress, Lauren. *Walking a Sacred Path*. New York: Berkeley Publishing Group, 1995.

Bondi, Roberta. *To Pray and to Love: Conversations on Prayer with the Early Church*. Minneapolis: Fortress Press, 1991.

Brueggemann, Walter. *Praying the Psalms*. Winona, MN: Saint Mary's Press, 1986.

Burrows, Ruth. *Guidelines for Mystical Prayer*. London: Burns & Oates, 2007.

Douglas-Klotz, Neil. *Prayers of the Cosmos: Meditations on the Aramaic Words of Jesus*. San Francisco: Harper, 1990.

Foster, Richard and James Bryan Smith. *Devotional Classics*. New York: Harper One, 1993.

Geitz, Elizabeth Rankin, Marjorie A. Burke, and Ann Smith, editors. *Women's Uncommon Prayers*. Harrisburg, PA: Morehouse Publishing, 2000.

Lewis, C. S. *Letters to Malcolm: Chiefly on Prayer*. New York: Houghton Mifflin Harcourt, 2012.

Louf, Andre. *Teach Us to Pray*. Cambridge, MA: Cowley, 1992.

Merton, Thomas. *Contemplative Prayer*. New York: Doubleday/Image, 2009

Schmidt, Joseph F. *Praying Our Experiences*. Frederick, MD: De la Salle Christian Brothers, 2008.

Chapter 6

Imagination, Art, and Play: The Practice of Possibility

An ethical imagination needs to play . . . ,
to ensure it liberates, animates and enlarges our response to the other.
Imagination needs to be able to laugh with the other as well as to suffer.
Richard Kearney, *The Wake of Imagination*

What If?

Two remarkable and simple words offer a wonderful doorway into the realm of the Holy. Poets and children spend entire days devoted to these two words. Many of the most amazing inventions, and all of the best bits of wondrous possibility begin with the words "What if . . . ?" What if today I chose to be still first instead of running headlong into the day attempting to accomplish everything on my list? What if I honored that internal nudge to call on a sick friend as if that nudge were God's voice in me? What if instead of certainty I chose the path of curiosity to see where it leads today? If we are to come close to God and truly enter into the heart of the spiritual life we will need to constantly cultivate our sense of "What if . . . ?" and open ourselves to new possibilities. We will need to become travelers from the known, expected, and ordinary to the unknown, unexpected, and extraordinary. We need to expand our capacity for holy imagination.

Many of the most trusted spiritual writers share their love for God and their ability to cultivate a lifelong sense of God's abiding presence through the realm of imagination and the expansion of the sense of wonder. Each one speaks of a particular pathway to the interior life that can be accessed through visualization and the cultivation of images in our mind's eye. That is not to say we are working on creating fiction, but rather expanding our capacity to consider what is not immediately before our eyes. The French existential philosopher Jean Paul Sartre defined the imagination as the particular human ability "to think of what is not." What we are talking about is a capacity that allows us to consider possibilities that we have not yet seen.

This unseen we are seeking to explore includes both the spiritual realms of the holy and the interior realms of psyche, beliefs, and emotions that if we do not call them into conscious awareness will remain hidden and unexplored and we will be the poorer for having neglected them. Many of us operate under unexamined assumptions and from painful memories that unconsciously dictate current behaviors. We carry wounds and prejudices that direct our behavior in a way that falls short of the grace that God invites us to incarnate. God desires our transformation and freedom from these burdens, and lovingly asks to be allowed to enter into the deepest parts of our hearts and minds to accomplish that healing.

There are those who feel the spiritual realm is completely distinct from the human interior world while others assert that they are intertwined. It seems that to be human is to dwell on the threshold of many possible ways of being in the world and many streams of influence; internal and external, physical and non-physical. By using the gifts of prayer and meditation in addition to other creative practices we can begin to bring ourselves in touch with God who is the creative loving center of all reality. As Christians we confess that Jesus is the incarnation of both worlds, fully human and fully divine. He speaks with angels and with humans. He casts out demons and stills the winds. When questioned by legal and military authorities of the day he acknowledged that his kingdom was not of this world (John 18:36). He alludes to his Lordship of the kingdom of heaven; a spiritual realm with manifestations in the physical world. We too are called to be citizens of both realms, though the physical realm often has a much more obvious claim upon us.

Part of the gift of imaginative work is that it gives us the opportunity to develop our ability to suspend our disbelief and to visualize things which are beyond the realm of the eyes. Most of us naturally dwell in a culture of disbelief. "If I can't see it or touch it, it cannot be real." If it seems too good to be true it usually is, but as our imagination and willingness to draw near to God in subtler ways develops, so too does our ability to see beyond the realm of the eyes. Instead of just thinking about God's love for us we can see in our mind's eye ourselves actually being embraced by that love in whatever shape our imagination chooses for it to take shape. Having had a prayerful experience of that love in our mind's eye we now can deepen our trust of that reality. The skills of suspending disbelief and visualizing the invisible compose perhaps some of the most essential tasks of faith. "Now faith is the assurance of things hoped for, the conviction of things not seen" (Hebrews 11:1). Our spiritual mothers and fathers each took the laughable leap of faith when they first heard a still small voice and imagined it might be the very voice of God. Picture Abraham in the ancient desert looking up at the night sky and hearing some voice, a voice that was not his own, calling him to leave home. This interior holy nudge urged him to go and follow a soul whisper from a voice he was just beginning to recognize as God. It was a voice which he might have shaken off the first time he heard it, but something about the quality and power of the pull caused him to wonder, "What if this is how God speaks?"

Consider Moses, a simple shepherd watching his father in law's flock of sheep, when he smells smoke and decides to turn and take a look at some strange phenomenon of nature in a burning bush. He notes that nothing else nearby is on fire, and that the fire is not consuming the bush. He could have shrugged it off as just an oddity of the desert and kept on walking with his sheep. Instead he allowed himself to be drawn in closer and in doing so he crossed the threshold between the physical world and the spiritual realm. One can almost hear him asking the internal "what if . . ." question. For his courage and willingness to be astonished he is rewarded with a divine encounter which launched the liberation of the people of God.

Imagined Shadows

Not all imaginings are blessed encounters. We can imagine nightmarish terrors, and easily fill ourselves with fictional delusions. Some of these imaginative encounters can serve as messengers much like the ghosts of Christmas past who haunt Ebenezer Scrooge in Charles Dickens's *A Christmas Carol*. They are painful provocateurs who call us to repent from self-serving greed to generosity and compassion. Other imaginings can lead us down deadly paths of self-destruction. No sooner had Moses accomplished the liberation of the Israelites and gone up the mountain to listen to God than the people grew impatient awaiting his return and imagined that a calf, made out of their own melted jewelry, might take God's place.

The story of the golden calf presents the question: if we begin to wander into this realm of imagination, how are we to know if what we sense, or hear, or feel, or imagine is of God? As a pastor and a person of faith, I have long wrestled with this question on behalf of others and in my own spiritual life. In working with this issue in a small group, one of our members was a scientist who had a rich and beautiful life of prayer. From time to time, she felt that she might have heard God speaking to her. She was willing to ask the "what if" question and allow that what she was hearing might indeed be divine guidance. At the same time her well-trained rational mind offered up the same question with a different twist, "what if it is all made up and you are just hearing what you want to hear?" The leader of our group responded with a wonderful question and one that is grounded in scripture. She invited my friend to consider whether what she was hearing in her inner self was drawing her closer to God, or turning her away from God. The first letter of John counsels believers in much the same manner (1 John 4:1). He tells the beloved community of believers not to accept every spirit, but to test the spirits to see whether or not they are from God. If they confess Christ as a divine incarnation, that is if they lead you toward the God of love, grace, and forgiveness as manifest in Christ, then they are from God. Ours is a God willing to go to any length to catch our attention and at the same time choosing to remain mysteriously hidden. Who are we to say that God could not use the words of a friend, the visions of dreams, the whispers of the heart, or the luminous light of a star to show us where to find the Holy which we seek.

Interior Realities

Another gifted teacher of the practice of holy imagination was Teresa of Avila. She was wise in discerning those imaginings which led us towards God and those which seek to inhibit and create barriers to the blessings which God seeks to offer us in the spiritual life. She begins the introduction to her marvelously creative and seminal work *Interior Castle* with these words. *"There is a secret place. A radiant sanctuary.*

As real as your own kitchen. More real than that."[1] She goes on to describe in vivid detail comforts like velvet feather beds, sumptuous intoxicating wines, and long sought-after clarity for seekers. In just a few sentences Teresa summons us into the interior realm of the holy through the door of our imagination. Perhaps better than any other writer of her time, Teresa actively engages our sense of wonder and creative visualization in order to lay out a map of the challenges of the interior spiritual life which she portrays as vipers, lizards, and lions, and draws us toward the lap of the Beloved who waits for us with loving welcome in the innermost chamber of our hearts. In these first words she also inadvertently acknowledges and dismisses one of the questions that troubles the life of those engaged in spiritual explorations: the age-old question "if I imagine it, is it real?" Teresa assures us that the riches and pitfalls which we encounter in the world of interior images are as real as anything revealed in the outer world of the five senses.

I join Teresa in this assertion with an example from my own experience. In the spring of 1988 I had been studying Morton Kelsey's book, *Caring,* with a small group at my church. In it he wrote of needing some help beyond himself and so he turned inward using his imagination to visit what he calls his soul room.[2] I was captivated by this idea and by his confidence that we can encounter both the holy and our innermost selves by becoming still and allowing the images to arise naturally. I began to wonder if I had a soul room, and if I did what it might look like. I prayed that God might show me a meeting place where I could know God better and see what God might want to show me about myself and the life of the Spirit. It was a quiet afternoon and I chose to be in prayer outside. After some period of stillness and quiet and by gently holding the questions about my soul room I began to see in my mind a grassy hillside with a door. I entered the door and found a cozy room with a fireplace, table, candle, and benches. There was a welcoming presence there and I knew I was home. I was having a hard time imagining Christ there. I couldn't help but wrestle with the exact features and struggle with the variety of images that I had encountered over the years and none of them worked in my mind's eye. Gradually a radically alternative image of Christ began to emerge. She was the suffering servant and triumphant lioness present with me to offer wisdom and guidance usually through well timed and holy questions. Behind her in another interior room I could see a flutter of moving color and light creating things, and weaving. This was the Spirit. In a deeper inner chamber set apart from this room was a luminous whirlwind of swirling energy and intense light and love. This I imagined was God. I was afraid to go into that room. Not the fear of shame, but the recognition of my tiny fragile humanness in the presence of such astonishing power and pure Being.

This conscious imaginative prayer continued and I was shown through images that arose in my mind's eye a number of defenses that I relied on that God was inviting me to surrender. As I released each one God offered a replacement far superior to that which I had been clinging. Finally I was invited to come very close to God. It was like being near a blazing fire but not suffering from the heat. A hand emerged from the center of God's being and withdrew a tiny flickering flame which was extended to me and placed inside my heart. This seemed almost too much for me. I began to jump into my critical mind and start to ask where is this all coming from? How could God be giving me a part of God's self? Was I going just a bit crazy here? As I asked these questions the tiny flame God had given me began to flicker and go out. I was so sad. I had questioned this gift to death. Without judgment or a word at all God's hand reached inward again, drawing out another flame and extending it into my heart again. I was relieved and joyful. It was as though God was saying, "you can question this to death, and you can examine the life out of it, but I will offer it again, and again, and again. You cannot quench the fire I place in you."

I came into my conscious mind with tears streaming down my face, aware that I had been in a privileged space created both of my imagination and of the grace of God. I know that it had been a meditation, but it was also real in the way that Teresa and others have written about encounters with the holy. To this day I am blessed and forever changed by an act of prayerful imagination where God could speak to me in images. In times of doubt or spiritual fatigue God invites me to return to the reassurance of what I saw, heard, and experienced in that day of meditation. It is a real touchstone of personal truth that continues to ground and guide my relationship with God. Others have shared similar experiences that have come both in prayer and in dreams. The impact of these encounters, though they did not happen in the physical realm are undeniably real.

Bringing Our Whole Selves Before God

How might one begin to cultivate such a practice and engage the imagination for spiritual formation? Here a faithful friend, Ignatius of

Loyola, is a good guide. Ignatius, with a small group of friends, founded the Society of Jesus or the Jesuit order, whose focus and aim was to be contemplatives in action. Through his own journaling and prayer he came to develop a series of exercises that would deepen one's relationship with God. For centuries the exercises were given as a series of long retreats, but now many utilize them in daily life. The especially helpful part of Ignatius's exercises is his utilization of imagination. In one exercise he invites us to imagine the world from God's viewpoint. When we seek that viewpoint our sense of compassion and love are expanded. The second part of the exercises has us using our imagination to place ourselves in a scripture story using all of our senses to fully enter into it. If we are reading the passage about the feeding of the five thousand, we take an imaginative look at the surrounding landscape. We feel the heat, notice the landmarks, and hear the murmur of the crowd. We smell the air and the people and animals around us. In our mind's eye we begin to notice that our clothing might be homespun and a bit scratchy, and our sandals are perhaps tight and our feet tired. We allow ourselves to feel the hunger as the dinner hour approaches and we engage the inner tension as we try to decide whether to stay with the teacher or go home for a meal. We listen and see what other words Jesus might have said. We are not just reading about this story we are meeting Christ. We visualize every aspect of the encounter and allow it to take root within us.

In this type of practice we are seeking to make the invisible visible, and seeking to find a new vocabulary to articulate a holy mystery. One of the most remarkable traits of humans is that we can use symbols to represent ideas, and images to convey thoughts and feelings. Archeologists have found testimony to rituals, hunts, and important life events such as births and deaths on cave walls for thousands of years. The world of images connects us to the depths within us and the depths of the holy, and the creation of art in a posture of contemplation often is useful for getting past the guards our conscious rational minds put up.

Encountering Resistance

Gerald May, psychiatrist, author and co-founder of the Shalem Institute which trains spiritual directors, writes of this tension between our desire to connect with God and the many resistances we have against that same unity. In his book *Will and Spirit*, May writes eloquently of the human tension between self-control—our wills—and the trajectory of the deepening spiritual life which is ultimately a relinquishment or self-losing experience.[3] We are aching to connect with the deep love of God and we know that we will be changed in that encounter, so we unconsciously resist entering into the interior space and create barriers which inhibit that transcendent experience with God. This is one of the places where art comes in handy. The process of art making and reflecting on our creations has a tremendous power to jump the fences that the logical self-protective side of our brains put in place.

Biblical scholar and writer Walter Wink combines a love of scripture study, brain research, and creativity in his small book *Transforming Bible Study*. Research about the functions of the right and left hemispheres of the brain inform Wink's style of Bible study. This research indicates that the left side of the brain interprets temporal relations, linear time, analytical, logical and sequential thinking, speech, and math, while the right side guides our synthesis of information, the creative process, depth perception, dreams, meditation, art, and innovation.[4] Experiments in education that blended increased art classes along with math and science led to higher math and science scores. Researchers had found that this exposure to creativity was allowing students to bring more of their brain, especially the parts of intuition and "hunch." This synthesis of right and left brain allowed students to pull together complex ideas and information in new ways at a higher level. That is to say, for the most part, we are usually heavily reliant on the logical and linear sides of our brain, but with art making and creative play both sides are engaged and insights and synthesis are more readily accessible. Rather than offering God only one part of our minds with creativity and imagination we can bring our whole selves to God in prayer.

If we follow Wink's method of Bible study we are invited not only to become familiar with the context of the passage we are studying, but, much like Ignatius, to try to make personal connections with the text. If, for example, we are working with the story about the lame man at the pool from John 5, we are invited to hear deeply Jesus' question in verse 6, "Do you want to be made well?" The man in the Bible passage does not respond immediately to Jesus's question, but instead makes numerous excuses about his situation. Wink's process calls us to examine the excuses we make about the situation of our lives and our well-being. What would it cost us to be well? When have we felt that we were kept down by a situation beyond our control? We imagine ourselves in the place of the lame man and make as many connections as we can with our own lives. Finally, when Jesus tells him to take up his mat and walk we hear it as a call in our own lives. We experience both the relief and the power of Jesus's command to live life differently and whole. The process that Wink adds to Bible study is a creative response to the study of the text. So with this passage we might work with clay or do a simple drawing of our inner brokenness being healed. We make a visual representation of an inner reality and thereby bring it to consciousness where we can offer it up in prayer and begin the process of having it fully integrated into our lives.

I experienced the power of this type of integration and revelation when I was studying on a retreat with Walter Wink at Stoney Point Retreat Center in New York. I had entered seminary and concluded my first year. I thought I had given all that I could give over to God. The group was led through a study on a passage about surrender and healing. I honestly can't remember the exact passage, but it may have been the story of the rich young ruler. What I do remember was what happened when we were each given a small chunk of clay and told simply to play with it. We were invited to pray about what parts of ourselves we need to surrender in order to follow Christ. I couldn't imagine anything else I had left to give up. I had left my home, my family, my job, most of my furniture. What else could there be? As I played with the clay something began to take shape. I could feel a small body beginning to emerge. I squished and rolled and patted some more, and wings added themselves to the little bird body. I was not intentionally creating anything; just allowing my hands to play and form a shape as I prayed about what to relinquish. Finally, a small clay bird was sitting in my hand. I had no idea what to make of it. I didn't own a bird, and was unsure why this had emerged from the clay and prayer. After a period of simply sitting with this little creation I gradually realized that what it represented was my spirit. I had given God all the external markings of my independence, but I had not yet fully surrendered my entire heart and innermost self. This stunning realization led me to a profound examination of my sense of fully trusting God, consenting anew to fully give to God the whole of my being.

Whenever art making is mentioned so many folks immediately respond with the defense, "But I'm no good at art." It is important to bear in mind that the art making we are talking about here is far more about process than it is about product. We aren't really trying to produce anything, but rather give our full attention to God and to cultivate a variety of ways to listen for and hear from God. This is not about making fine art, but rather fine tuning the soul to hear its Creator's voice. Simply letting the colors move across the page, or even doing it with our eyes closed and then filling in the shapes as we hold a prayerful question can deepen our attention to God. Visual art is not the only expression available to us either. Simple Haiku poem prayers where we work to distill our heart's longing and praise into the familiar five-seven-five syllable lines can be a great practice too. Later in this chapter there will be an exercise in writing a dialogue with God which invites us to use our imagination to both listen and write down what we hear the voice of God inside saying to us. Collage is an especially accessible art prayer form. Gathering images, words, and shapes that give voice to our inner longings allows us to sit with our attention on the Holy One can be both restful and revealing.

Time to Play

There is a playful quality about this type of art making and imagining that is essential. In fact, Stuart Brown MD, who is recognized by many as an authority on the topic of play, suggests that play is a critical part of our well-being and wholeness as humans. Even if a desire to serve and love God is at the heart of all our efforts, if there is not a balance with play, even love can become drudgery. The poetic book Ecclesiastes reminds us that balance is essential to our lives.

> For everything there is a season, and a time for every matter under heaven: a time to be born, and a time to die; a time to plant, and a time to pluck up what is planted; a time to kill, and a time to heal; a time to break down, and a time to build up; a time to weep, and a time to laugh; a time to mourn, and a time to dance; a time to throw away stones, and a time to gather stones together; a time to embrace, and a time to refrain from embracing; a time to seek, and a time to lose; a time to keep, and a time to throw away; a time to tear, and a time to sew; a time to keep silence, and a time to speak; a time to love, and a time to hate; a time for war, and a time for peace. (Ecclesiastes 3:1-8)

Just as there is a time for serious work and study, so there is a time and a necessity for rest and play in the spiritual life. In the center of the commandments God gave to God's people is a command to remember the Sabbath and keep it holy. Whether you take the list from Exodus 20 or Deuteronomy 5, we are given a command to lay down our work on one of every seven days. Exodus tells us that we pattern ourselves after God who also rested on the seventh day, and Deuteronomy tells us that we do so in order to remember that we were once slaves in Egypt, but that the grace of God has set us free. We are invited to live fully into this freedom and joy. Rest and play are a central part of that equation.

Opportunities for play create occasions for learning new ways of thinking and being in community. We call it recreation because it does in fact help us to be re-created, rested, restored. Play as a spiritual practice is fully accepting the abundance of life that God has given us and thoroughly enjoying it. It is also a declaration of faith in the promises that God makes to provide for our wellbeing. Researchers who study play say that as we play we move through a flow of positive experiences, "anticipation, surprise, pleasure, understanding, strength, and poise."[5] Those are all things God desires for us and gifts that come through play. Ask anyone who has been part of a team building experience on a ropes course or had the fun of playing with a youth group if they didn't learn a great deal about themselves, one another, and perhaps God simply from the experience of playing.

Group play is certainly one avenue of a practice that is renewing for the spirit, and individual play can also be a form of prayer and an expression of gratitude to God. The psalms are full of calls to make a joyful noise to the Lord. We serve a God who desires goodness and joy for us, but sometimes we get very serious trying to serve that God. I recall being very devout and earnestly seeking to follow God my senior year at seminary. I was nearly paralyzed in my inability to discern God's path for my ministry, so I called on one of my theology professors. He listened with compassion to my overly zealous passionate willingness to go anywhere and do anything for God and finally he asked me the life changing question, "What would give you delight?" I was stunned. Delight? How could this be part of the equation? I thought following God was serious business. I told him my thoughts and he smiled. He went on to suggest that the God who created me had also created the particular joys and resonance within me so that I might be drawn to that which also blessed the world. When was I the happiest? What did I love to do? Why couldn't I do that in the service of God? This was wild new liberating territory, and on a very deep level it echoed the call of the Exodus. God does not desire that we live in soul crushing slavery, but rather calls us to service and obedience in joy. With this new understanding I was able to move forward remembering what I loved and discover ministry that was both renewing, life giving, and faithful.

One of the often overlooked significant gifts that play offers us is the opportunity to experience and survive loss and failure.

Three strikes and you're out—but not out forever, just until the next inning. The balloon bursts unexpectedly and there is shock and perhaps tears, but also sometimes laughter and surprise. The end of the slide comes too suddenly and we land with a hard smack on the ground. Now we get to decide if we are going to live in fear of slides forever or conquer that monster and try to land on our feet. The very act of playing is an exercise in resilience and choosing to try again.

All too often we lose sight of that which gives us joy as we take on adult responsibilities. We think that play is for children, but Stuart Brown argues that play is essential in all ages of life. Remember jumping in leaf piles in the fall, or splashing in puddles in the rain? Those were small acts of joy and praise to the Creator of trees and sky. We can add a moment of grace to our days by simply stopping work for a moment to gaze out the window and lift up a prayer of gratitude for all that we see. Or better yet, get up from the desk to walk outside and admire creation as a perfect way to add the practice of play to our daily pattern. Just as the early church had set hours for prayer perhaps there could be a joy filled revolution in set hours for play.

Recently I came to the place in my work day where I had become tired and stuck. Rooting through my desk for paper clips I came across a worn down and broken set of colored pencils. In a desperate need to feel productive I decided I would sharpen them and laughed as I posted on Facebook, "I have come to the place in my work day when the only sensible thing to do is to sharpen my colored pencils. So if anyone wants to come and color, I am all ready." Not fifteen minutes later a congregation member popped in the door and said she was there to color. We had a wonderful short break, got to know each other better, and enjoyed a tiny service of worship in color and laughter. There were a dozen other comments from folks aching to play. It is a delight to know that God not only gives us permission, but even a commandment to stop, rest, play, and rejoice.

These spiritual practices of imagination, art, and play are gifts God has given us to welcome us into God's own presence. "Unless you change and become like children . . ." goes the verse from Matthew's gospel. Perhaps Christ was referring to cultivating a playful trusting spirit of simplicity and not knowing all the answers, and also to being willing to step out in faith by asking, "What if . . . ?"

SAMPLE EXERCISES

Imagining Your Inner Realm

Both Teresa of Avila and Morton Kelsey suggest that there is an interior place for connection with God. What might yours look like? Is it a stately sanctuary or wild place? Is it occupied? Is someone waiting there for you? Are there barriers to getting in? Is something blocking the way? What do you find when you look inside?

Writing: Dialogue with God

Writing a dialogue with God is much like writing a play. In this exercise you will be writing both your voice and what your inner voice hears God speaking to you. While many people bristle at the idea of God speaking to them, this is where imagination comes in. We know God from our life experiences, and from the teaching of scripture. We have an inner sense of the divine because we are made in God's image. Practice quieting your inner skeptic and simply allow the writing process to take place without examining it too severely.

Take some time and choose a place where you can be still and uninterrupted for at least 30 minutes. Have paper and something to write with on hand. Begin in stillness noticing your breath and inviting God to be present with you in this time of creative prayer. Begin to write about things that are on your heart, or on your mind and see if there is a theme or question that is arising. Return to the stillness and again invite God to be present with you. When you first begin this type of practice you will have to press past all the resistances that arise. Try to get at least 5 or 6 exchanges down on paper. You might begin your dialogue in this way:

Betsy: "God, I need your wisdom on this matter. I am wondering/ concerned about/needing . . ."

God: "Hello, Betsy, it is good to be with you . . ."

Keep writing what you hear in your heart and what you want to say to God. Often God responds with a question rather than a clear answer. Try not to edit what you say and what you take down. Trust yourself and God who wants so deeply to connect with you. When you have finished writing conclude with a prayer of gratitude for the chance to be with God.

Imagining: Full Sensory Scripture reading.

Begin with an interior posture of prayer. Allow your intention to be one of connecting with God and seeing what God wants to show you

in this passage from scripture. Choose a passage with human interaction and narrative. As you read, begin to consider which characters
you connect with and what their vantage point might be. For the purposes of explaining this practice we will be using Mark 2: 1-12 in which
Jesus heals a paralytic. Read the passage several times through so that
you are familiar with the movements of the story. You might even
take some notes with questions beside them. The passage from Mark
begins in a very crowded house. Pause there and place yourself in the
crowd. Are you near the front of the room? Are you pressed to one of
the walls? Are you on tiptoe outside the door? What is the energy of the
crowd like? Are they excited, anxious, fearful? How do you feel being
this close to Jesus? Perhaps in this story you are one of the friends and
you have brought someone to be healed by Christ, or perhaps you are
the paralytic. Find your place in the story first. What smells do you
notice? Has someone been cooking recently? Can you smell the clay
and dryness of the dirt walls and the straw roof? What is the crowd
doing and saying as people take apart a piece of the roof to let a man
down on a mat? How do you feel witnessing this? Can you see Jesus
from your vantage point? What does his face tell you about how he is
experiencing this? Jesus speaks the words, "Your sins are forgiven."
How do you experience these words? What emotions arise for you in
this interaction? There is an argument between Jesus and the scribes.
What are they fighting about? Jesus tells the paralytic to, "get up, take
up your mat and go to your home" What is the tone of his voice? The
man is getting up to walk. What has passed between him and Jesus?
How have you been changed by what you have seen? Bring your time
of visualization to a close with prayer of gratitude for this encounter
with Jesus.

Visual: Prayer Mandala

Mandalas are sacred circles. While the origin of the word is Hindu,
people of all faiths use this simple shape to hold prayers, intentions,
and conversations with God. Mandalas can be any size at all, but the
images are held in the circle. For this practice we will need paper of any
color and a variety of colors to draw with. Colored pencils, crayons, or
pastels work well. It is also helpful to have a round shape to trace such
as a dinner plate. With this exercise the intention is again simply to
allow yourself to be available to what God wants to show you. Take
time to prepare your space with your materials, and pre-draw a circle
on the paper you have chosen. Allow your whole self to be present and

available to God as you begin. Take a few minutes to be still within yourself and become aware of God's presence with you. Let yourself be drawn to any color to begin. There is no wrong way to make a mandala. Just begin making marks inside the circle. It is not necessary to make recognizable images. Just choosing the colors and making the marks is your prayer. This practice is about being fully present to color and shape. Sometimes images arise. Allow them to come and capture them if you can. Bit by bit your mandala will fill in. Go slowly and savor the time of being still. It is not necessary to fill the whole space inside the circle. This is a practice in which we are just playing with color, shape, and texture. Some will be geometric, others will be free form. If drawing your own mandala seems daunting you might begin with Suzanne Fincher's book, *Coloring Mandalas for Insight, Healing, and Self Expression.*[6] After you have completed your mandala take time to enjoy it. Turn it and view it from different vantage points. It may have a new orientation that is even more powerful than the one in which it was originally drawn. It can also be a rich experience to try to name the mandala. If this were a work of art what would you call it? When you are done appreciating your work lift it up as an offering to God.

Pray, Play, Walk

This walk can be done solo, with a friend, or even with a dog. The intention for this walk is to see and take joy in God's creation. You might simply walk, or you might take some props like bubbles, a ball, or a camera. You can do this walk in any setting urban or natural since it is about seeing and appreciating. As you walk allow your heart to lead you on the path. Go about twice as slow as you normally would. Remember this is not about achievement, but being present with God. Allow yourself to look up, stop, and be pulled in new directions. So often we walk with intense purpose focused straight ahead or even eyes down and miss the beauty around us. What are you seeing that you might have missed if you walked more quickly? You could take photos and write a prayer of gratitude for what you have seen. What parables of the spiritual life are being revealed to you? Where is life breaking forth? What season is it in the year? How does that parallel or contrast the season it is in your soul? Are there broken places that you see? What is the prayer of those places, people, or plants? If you encounter people on your walk what is your prayer for them? How is God at work in what you are seeing? If you happen to have a dog and a ball along take time to play and notice the joy it brings. If you brought the bubbles along stop and blow them. Savor the iridescent short lived sparkle. What childhood memories arise?

FOR FURTHER READING

Teresa of Avila. *The Interior Castle.* Translated by Mirabai Starr. New York: Riverhead Books, 2003

Nancy Azara. *Spirit Taking Form.* York Beach, ME: Red Wheel/Weiser, LLC, 2002.

Stuart Brown and Christopher Vaughan. *Play: How It Shapes the Brain, Opens the Imagination, and Invigorates the Soul.* New York: Penguin Group, 2009.

Julia Cameron. *The Artists Way: A Spiritual Path to Higher Creativity.* New York: Penguin Putnam, 1992.

Suzanne Fincher. *Coloring Mandalas for Insight, Healing, and Self Expression.* Boston, MA: Shambhala, 2000.

Morton Kelsey. *Caring.* Minneapolis, Minnesota: Augsburg Publishing House, 1980.

Cathy Malchiodi. *The Soul's Palette: Drawing on Art's Transformative Powers for Health and Well-Being.* Boston, MA: Shambhala, 2002.

Michael Sullivan, *Windows on the Soul.* Harrisburg, PA: Morehouse Publishing, 2006.

Christine Valters Paintner and Betsy Beckman. *Awakening the Creative Spirit: Bringing the Arts to Spiritual Direction.* Harrisburg, PA: Morehouse Publishing, 2010.

Elizabeth-Anne Vanek. *Image Guidance.* New York: Paulist Press, 1992.

Walter Wink. *Transforming Bible Study.* Nashville, TN: Abingdon Press, 1980.

Chapter 7

శ

Virtue: The Practice of Integrity

How do introspection and self-observation differ?
The former is narrow and somewhat cannibalistic:
one tends to consume one's own substance within a repetitive circle of experience.
Introspection tends to increase one's misery.
Self-observation is something else again: it is watered by ancient teachings . . .
And undertaken in order to be equal to a task that requires more than
one could otherwise give.
Roger Lipsey, *Parabola*, Fall, 1997 (51)

Virtue refers to what a person would be if his or her nature were fully realized: a quality of wholeness. The spiritual person understands that human wholeness consists both of a firm self-esteem and a willing self-surrender to the Mystery in which we live and move and have our being. Virtue is the tradition's word for human response to the call of Divine Being. It rests in sensing something desirable and out of reach (the Mystery that is God) and risking to move toward it, knowing that God is also moving toward us. Virtue is both acquired (by our practice) and infused (God's gifts of grace), meaning that we cooperate with God in forming our character for the work of love. Acquiring virtue means growing in our capacity to choose the good, not simply in one good choice, but by the habitual training of the will toward and with God.

Integrity means being whole, having the focused attention which early Christians called purity of heart. The opposite is being constantly pulled in many directions, grabbing quickly at the best bang for the buck or the most exciting transitory option, and eventually forgetting altogether those interior standards by which life gains meaning and purpose. Virtue refers to a person's character, one's capacity to act according to interior values, the vital strength at the core of one's being. If I ask myself what I am most likely to do, given any particular set of circumstances, the answer will reveal the current quality of my character. For example, a test was once given to a group of seminary students who had been told to hurry across campus for an important event in another building. Along the route they must walk past a person who had clearly been beaten up. Most of the students passed right by in their haste to get to the assigned building. Only one or two stopped to care for the distressed person. The students were responding out of existing inner habits, partly blind obedience to authority and partly a sense that their studies were more important than an unknown person in need. The response we offer to life events is guided by the current shape of our character.

Jesus says that what comes out of a person reveals their virtuous character or its absence (Matt. 15:10-11). Yet sometimes "spiritual people" neglect the inner formation so important in establishing virtue. This chapter is about the lifelong task of shaping and refining personal character, an essential component of spiritual growth. That is also to say that the chapter is about becoming whole and holy, a person of virtue. Although the focus is on individual inner work, this practice also has significant social dimensions because it strongly affects all our interactions with the world. C. S. Lewis observes that in each choice and action, we are either moving toward or away from God.[1] So no moment is too small for practice, and everything matters. Without this practice, we may find our souls so stuffed with minor disturbances that the channels to and from God become blocked.

The Importance of Thoughts

The fundamental way to the acquisition of virtue and the formation of character is through our *thoughts*. At first we may think it odd that thoughts should be so important. But consider Jesus's Sermon on the Mount (found in the Gospel of Matthew, chapters 5-7). Again and again Jesus says, "You have heard that . . . , but I tell you. . . ." The shift

Jesus makes in these instructions is always the shift from a particular action to a mode of response that involves *how we think*. For example, we have heard not to kill, but Jesus adds that *"everyone who is angry with his brother shall be liable to judgment"* (Matt. 5:22). Thoughts have a destructive power no less than actions.

Reflecting on these verses, Augustine of Hippo discerns three basic steps in the commission of sin. (1) The first is the basic impulse, the idea appearing in our heads. There is no blame to this impulse; thoughts simply happen. The choice comes in what we do with the thought. (2) The second step can be called giving shelter to the thought, or entertaining it. Instead of letting it pass by, we may consider it, turn it over, and imagine how it might be. In some respects, this is the most dangerous moment, for once an idea takes root in our minds, it gains a certain hold on our attention. (3) It is then not far to the third step, which involves intention, taking pleasure in visualizing the idea, immersing oneself in it, embracing the thought as something to be taken up actively.[2]

Pause to reflect:
- *How have you noticed this progression from a simple thought to the next movement of giving it shelter in your own life? Can you imagine becoming aware of that first thought as an invitation to turn towards the Holy? Is it possible to allow those first impulsive negative and selfish jolts to lead you to God, rather than leading you to scold yourself or be shamed and enticed by the troubling thoughts?*
- *Take a moment to remember a time when a thought became an action which injured another. We all have them. Now visualize the Holy One coming to you and redirecting your energy and attention back to Love and mercy. How does the story change as you meditate on it in the presence of Divine Love?*

Note that sometimes the pleasure we may take in a thought is similar to that of a worn-out shoe, no longer able to provide real support or protection, but "comfortable" because familiar. For example, the idea that "I am stupid; I never get things right" may be one that I find myself courting time after time, though perhaps not fully consciously. Or I may court a thought like "That person always angers me, and I wish they would go away." These may be trivial thoughts, but when we regularly "feed" them by attending to them or mulling over them, they become quite dangerous to our soul's health. Augustine tells us that at each of these three points in reception of a thought, there is a choice, but each successive stage allows the thought to become more embedded, more compulsive, and more difficult to shake off until it blocks our reception of the goodness God would give us.

I am often astonished by how seldom people think of thoughts as involving spiritual work. We may find ourselves complaining continuously about coworkers or spouses, routinely feeling powerless and victimized by others, consistently thinking of ourselves as better than others, or allowing obsessions to take over our minds. Such patterns are very hurtful to spiritual growth and can undermine other spiritual practices. New habits of mind can be very freeing.

Today much of our thinking about prayer or communion with God seems focused on ignoring thoughts, refusing them, or suppressing them. From a psychological point of view we know that repression may eventually lead to a harmful outburst. What we may not see as clearly is that *forcing* thoughts away may well lead to a stunted soul, because what is needful for the soul is acknowledgement and *reformation* of the undesirable thoughts. The distinction made in the introductory quotation is important here. What is being suggested is not "introspection" which may often carry us into the second step Augustine describes. Instead, the practice of working with thoughts is "self-observation," in which we endeavor to stand at a little distance from our thoughts, noticing what and where they are trying to nudge us, observing them in the light of scripture, tradition, and spiritual reading, and endeavoring to reform them.

The practice recommended here is first to *notice* what it is that we regularly say to ourselves, our most common self-messages. Once we can see those thoughts clearly, we can employ tools to reform them in light of what we know about God. The practice is very simply described, though very difficult to sustain. We observe what the destructive thought is, then contrast it with what we know to be God's desire for wholeness, and seek through prayer to exchange destruction for reconciliation and renewal. The work is *not to eliminate personal will, but to retrain it into the paths of love.* Although this may now sound vague, as we consider in turn each of the major clusters of thoughts identified in early Christian tradition, reviewing potential alternatives, the pattern of the practice will become clearer.

Wisdom from Christian Tradition

The two most important collections of early Christian wisdom about *logosmoi*, thoughts (or better, disruptive thoughts and obsessive feelings), were those of Evagrius Pontus (fourth century CE) and John Cassian (360-435 CE), both of whom spent time in the Egyptian desert, living and talking with the wise men and women who had moved there to focus on God alone. Evagrius wrote *On Practice* and *Chapters on Prayer*, while Cassian wrote *Conferences* about specific conversations he held with various monks, and *Institutes* as a guide for the monasteries he later established in Gaul.[3] In later Christian history, Thomas Aquinas picked up and reworked this material into what he called the seven deadly sins, but his analysis carries a different tone and focus than the earlier work, which I find more helpful for the common life.

The desert wisdom about thoughts consists of eight clusters of the most troubling issues that surfaced for those living close to God (often in groups of "cells" near other monastics), and all eight were considered *distorted capacities for love*. The eight were further subdivided into three categories by which love can be distorted: excessive love, defective love, and perverted love. Because human nature does not change so very much, we should not be surprised to find how intimately we too experience similar troubled thoughts like those of the fourth century Christians. Each of eight issues are discussed separately below, and for those who find charts helpful, a summary of them all in chart form is included in this chapter. In the text, the thought clusters are discussed in order, starting from the least dangerous to the soul and leading toward the most dangerous.

Training Thoughts

Excessive Love

The first cluster falls into the category of **excessive love**, meaning love that is distorted by excessive attachment to something (other than God). The things in themselves are not wrong or evil; it is the exaggerated obsession with them that is problematic. They represent a flaw in the human capacity for desire, which itself is given by God to draw us toward Godself. But when desire is turned to lesser things in an exaggerated form, the way to God becomes blocked.

The Eight Clusters of Problem Thoughts and Possible Remedies

Excessive Love: Desire	Problem	Possible Remedies	Positive Form*
Food	too little; too much; picky	Create distance between desire and action; Combine fasting and meditation	Savoring
Sex	the other as object, to fulfill my needs	Better to try indirection—at first let law hold you; Silence good; also fasting–avoid the desired thing	Wonder/delight
Greed	think we "own" things; may start to worship money	Practice detachment & wise use of things; Focus on the memory of God, God's provision	Appreciation for the gifts of others
Defective Love: Will			
Anger	simmering resentment; focus on being wronged	Be aware that anger makes us blind, deluded; Practice vigilance, reconciliation, recollection	Energy for justice, for social change
Dejection	random sadness; depression; melancholy as a steady state	Stay in relationship; do one's best to amend faults and correct manners; Refrain from and redirect thoughts of putting oneself down; Resist morbid suffering; Remember Christ; Pray for hope and faith	Willingness to get help and to give it
Sloth/Acedia	a long, dry period; weariness of soul; vague uneasiness; sluggish mind	Not a time to make decisions; Rededicate self to work and relationships: manual labor especially helps; Be present to what is, rather than dissolve in memories or dreams	Endurance; patience
Perverted Love: Intellect			
Vainglory	take sole credit for good actions, or doing the right thing for the wrong reason; Opposite of dejection	Be watchful; then edit, redirect or change thoughts; Practice reverence and adoration; Return to prayer	Giving glory to God; be grateful in everything
Pride	I am "captain of my soul"; can determine my destiny and that of others	Begin again with control of thoughts; Pray; Be attentive to God's presence	Humility; Gratitude

*I am indebted to Sr. Dawn Mills, OSB, for these ideas about the positive form of thoughts. nv

Food and Drink

The desert monks came to see that food and drink can be a problem in three ways. One can desire too much food (more than the body needs), too little food (less than the body needs), or be picky about what one will eat or not eat. I value Mary Margaret Funk's observation that the practice of thoughts about food is not so much about food as it is about the practice of using food thought as a training tool.[4] Some of the other eight thoughts do not surface to our awareness quite so boldly, so food thoughts are a good place to start.

The practical remedy for excessive food thoughts is to eat only at meals, eat only what is served, and not desire an inappropriate quantity of food. We may realize at once that if we follow this pattern, we can fairly quickly get in touch with our thoughts about food: oh, I am hungry for a snack; I don't feel I can eat anything at meals; I can't eat anything with fat in it; and before you know it, I'm on the way to the cupboard or starving myself. I notice my thoughts about food and the train of thoughts they inspire. If I follow the food thought into action, I will soon find food is dominating my thoughts. Training my mind to notice and reform food thoughts removes the constant deliberation about what to eat and how much.[5] With fewer obsessive thoughts crowding my mind, I clear the channels for God's presence to me. The practice is to surrender my own thoughts, to bring to mind thoughts of God, and then to listen for God in this moment. A positive result of training the food thought is that we may find we savor what we do eat and drink appropriately, thanking God for bountiful provision.

Sex

Sex is also considered an excessive love, for desire itself can be a healthy thing, especially when directed toward God or as a genuine expression of ongoing mutual love. The excess arises when another is desired primarily to satisfy my own physical or emotional needs, or as an object onto which I have projected something I feel I need. Generally speaking, we know at once when inappropriate sexual thoughts arise (because they lure us to break existing commitments or force ourselves upon others). However, lust can be a powerful thought, returning again and again. Initially we may depend upon the letter and spirit of the laws and guidelines of our community, endeavoring not to entertain sex thoughts. The earlier the thought is caught on the screen of consciousness, the quicker we can gain control. With disturbing sex thoughts, avoiding the desired object as much as possible is wise, a kind of fasting from the other's presence. Cold showers, a glass of water, walking, prayer, and silence all are remedies to help restore us.

Chastity is the goal of bringing sex thoughts into appropriate place. Chastity is not necessarily celibacy, and for those not vowed to celibacy, chastity means enjoying sexual play within a long-term, established, and appropriate relationship, and accepting responsibility for the complexities of such a partnership. For single persons and those without partners, celibacy can eventually bring peace of mind and stronger spiritual energy. And, although we seldom find media attention to the joys of long-term partnerships, my own experience after thirty plus years of marriage is the considerable joy of living alongside someone I love, and together facing a number of interior "demons," able then to grow in mutual trust and wonder.

Greed

The third and last thought involving excessive love is greed, or obsession with things. Funk argues that amassing things is a learned behavior, not a natural instinct.[6] Cassian describes a chain of thoughts about greed, beginning with the thought that *what I have is insufficient for me,* proceeding to concerns about health, security, power and control, retirement, and so forth. In the process, one finds oneself lying, breaking promises, giving way to bursts of passions.[7] In effect, money becomes God to a person obsessed with greed. Like food and sex, the excessive love of things can never be satisfied, because the more one has, the more one wants. Especially with greed, nothing inside appears to allow a person to say, "This is enough."

The spiritual principle involved is that no human ever "owns" anything. God is owner and giver of all that exists, and whatever we have is given to us as steward. Some time ago, my husband reminded me that even our own children do not belong to us; they are simply given in trust, for our care and love. Love for our children is tested when they reach adulthood and generally move away from their childhood home to make their own life decisions. Genuine love learns to be ready for this relinquishment, willing to let go when the time comes, recognizing that eventually each person needs to learn to be responsible for his or her own life. In a similar way, it is well to practice willing relinquishment for everything we think is "ours."

The primary remedy for greed is to remember God, to bring ourselves back to the awareness of who God is, to trust that God will provide all that we need. Whenever we feel the desire for yet more, it is helpful to practice detachment, meaning awareness that all we have is simply on loan. Detachment does not mean that we care less, nor that we have no feelings for others and things; it simply means that we are learning to be free of dependence on illusory safety and security. Eventually with detachment will come a rich inner contentment that brings us joy. With this contentment, we are able to appreciate the gifts of others, as well as those given to us.

Defective Love

The second category of harmful thoughts is that of defective love: love that bears a serious flaw. Defective thoughts represent the failure of will to seek God. While the desert monastics understood the first group of thoughts as the misuse of the human power to embrace, they saw this next category of thoughts as a failure properly to use our human power of refusing. English lacks precise words to describe these two powers, producing only "lust" (concupiscence) for excessive embracing and "anger" (irascibility) for misplaced refusal, both of which fail to include the possible positive uses of the powers. The Cappadocian Fathers found that the embracing power was meant to be oriented primarily toward love of God, and the refusing power was meant to be used primarily against anything which would draw us away from God (what they called demons).[8] The point is that God made us as we are, so there must be some positive value to these basic impulses/powers. But those positive values can be distorted if we allow our thoughts to lead us into using these powers in destructive ways.

The thoughts of defective love are misuses of the will. Very often we think of will as essential to our individual rights, and usually we imagine it to be a forceful, assertive power. But will is not solely or even primarily "executive will," which is a function of the ego. There are other kinds of willing, one of which is the ability to *endure* through difficulties, and another of which leads toward "willingness" as that quality that enables us to *be there* for others. When will is defective, all of these positive powers deteriorate.

Anger

Anger can be a kind of simmering resentment or dwelling on an incident in which we feel we've been wronged. In today's world of such violence, it is well to ask to what extent our social structure itself contributes to inequalities that can magnify feelings of being wronged.

But anger seems to be so close to the surface in many of us at all social levels, perhaps especially when we feel our "rights" have been violated. Hurtful incidents may have happened years ago, yet when they have festered or not been worked through, they can remain a potent source of immediate anger. And because anger is often linked to a sense of helplessness to restore what we feel has been wrongly taken from us, anger often leads to explosive violence.

Anger is a powerful emotion, and can blind us. We lose perspective, and cease to be able to see others' points of view. The blindness of anger "disqualifies me for spiritual work, since I am out of relationship with myself, with others, and with God."[9] From this place of isolation from genuine relationship, we see the world only darkly. Rowan Williams observes that many of us have experienced betrayals, oppression, or experiences of abuse, and that one of the central spiritual issues is what we will do with those experiences. He suggests that in general there seem to be two primary options available: one is to become an abuser oneself, the other is to find oneself a victim over and over again. The drive toward one or another is such a common pattern that Williams suggests it can only be broken by an extraordinary event, which he finds in the crucifixion and resurrection of Christ.[10] In our behalf, Jesus refused to be an abuser and refused to accept victimization, as expressed in the power of his resurrection and the gift of the Holy Spirit. As a result, all of us are potentially freed of the vicious cycle of hurting or being hurt. A big part of the work in dealing with angry thoughts is our choice to accept or not accept the freedom offered to all in that Divine event.

Remedies for anger thoughts are vigilance (catch them early), reconciliation (befriend and pray for the person or persons who wounded you), solitude and recollection (release the blindness that confines you and move toward God). The anger energy can be used positively to work for justice and social change, to endure what cannot presently be changed, to pray for forgiveness. Sometimes anger is an appropriate response to personal or social abuse, supplying energy to resist victimization and to change what can be changed. However, even anger can be an enemy to wholeness/holiness if it eventually becomes the driving force of the ego. When things cannot be changed at present, the cultivation of a strong and centered position of endurance can be a positive use of anger energy. It can also be helpful to pray for the abuser, and entrust ultimate justice to God.

Dejection

Why should dejection be a harmful thought? It is not difficult to see why thoughts of excessive love and defective anger can be problematic. But dejection or sadness? Dejection can stand in opposition to anger, both connected to what we think our lives *ought* to be like, only to find it not so. Whereas anger directs inner disappointment outward to others, sadness directs the inner disappointment inwards against ourselves. Dejection is expressed in random sadness, melancholy as a steady state, impatience, a sort of acrid cynicism, and even despair. It may also be a chemical and physiological matter, requiring medical and therapeutic help.

With dejection, we believe we ourselves are somehow deficient, and that is why our life feels empty. Internally we may believe the issue is caused by the way we are made, we feel shame, and we see no hope of changing our inadequacy. We cease to see beauty, feel joy, taste goodness. The harm here is that God cares very much for each one of us, and there is no flaw that can reduce God's love. Yes, we are incomplete without God, but sadness assumes that the incompleteness can never be made whole, which is a refusal of God's generous outpouring to each and all.

Dejection is more than occasional sadness, more than sorrow for a loss. Dejection is a state of mind that persists for some time. It isolates a person from what is around them with feelings of hopelessness. It is an unwholesome sorrow which can seem to lower a cloud of discouragement around everything one is and does. For example, at one point in my life, I felt I was ready to shift my work into an institution, where I might express my giftedness with "a place to stand" and actually receive a regular salary for my work. Over a period of six months or more, several opportunities emerged which I faithfully followed up. I filled out all the paperwork, interviewed (even as a final round candidate), but no place seemed to want me. The rejections had something to do with my qualifications, although in most cases, the institution's own priorities changed during the search process, and I was not willing to twist myself into another shape to fit the new situation. As a result I spent a year or two feeling quite discouraged. I carried on with my previous work, but I felt a wrongness inside of myself. What was the problem that prevented me from moving forward as I hoped? Everything seemed bleak, and I was a little angry with God. But mostly I just felt sad, and that I had no way to make the change I felt I needed. Endurance helped a great deal and eventually the new opportunity emerged, not exactly the new job I had envisioned, but a return to school in a field which profoundly deepened my insights about the spiritual life.

Remedies for dejection thoughts begin with choosing to stay in relationship with others, even if one would prefer to withdraw. Focus on amending our own faults and manner, while refraining from and redirecting any and all thoughts of putting oneself down. It may also help to endeavor to attend more fully to the world around us, to look beyond the cloud of discouragement to rediscover the beauty and wonder of the created world. Finally, if possible, catch the dejection thought early and offer it at once in prayer to Christ. Notice the first impulse to dejection. Then, right away remind yourself that if God loves you so fully, who are you to call God wrong? Try to live into *this moment* as a person loved by God just as you are.

Dejection can eventually cause one to consider hurting oneself, so willingness to seek help is very important. Thoughts come and go, but we are more than our thoughts. When we are genuinely present to what actually is (and can break out of our cloud of dejection to see it), we come to be aware of a dynamism filling all times and places in this amazing world of ours. A friend can help us stay hopeful, even in the darkness. The positive form of this thought is the willingness to get help and to offer help.

Sloth/Acedia

The Greek word *acedia* has generally been translated as sloth, but that is not quite an accurate rendering of the term. *Acedia* was called the "noonday devil" by the desert monastics, occurring often in the "middle" times—middle of day, middle of week, middle of life course. It is a kind of weariness of the soul, a distaste for all that has sustained one for so long. One might have a bad mood that persists, perhaps leading to a rejection of the whole spiritual project, and even a desire to leave a long-time commitment to work or a relationship. A vague uneasiness accompanies a sluggish mind. One feels no energy to fight this thought which brings dislike and disgust. The irony and terror of *acedia* is that it usually appears just when current commitments are beginning to be beneficial to the soul, which is not a time to make important decisions. The best remedy is to rededicate oneself to work and relationships, and to be present to what is, rather than to one's dreams and fantasies. Manual labor helps, as may tears of compunction, praying to God for release from this terrible affliction. Perhaps this thought is a surge of the ego, competing with your long discipline, insisting on taking back control of your inner thoughts. *Acedia,* just as anger and dejection, is a defect of the will. So enlist your will, with God's help, to pass through this time.

Before we leave this section, it is important to note what defective love is and is not. Many of us have been told when children that we were not to be angry, not to be sad, not to be lazy. The practice of control of thoughts is not about following hard and fast rules, nor about social acceptability. It is not an insistence never to have certain feelings. It is rather an acceptance that as humans, we will no doubt have thoughts that disturb our inner harmony; but we do not need to engage nor enlarge those thoughts. By attending to our thoughts, we come to notice patterns in our thinking that block our ability to center our lives upon God. No one can tell us where we need to focus our practice at any given moment, because only we know what is arising interiorly to trouble our inner peace. The control of our thoughts is about moving toward a life of awareness and clarity, and becoming capable of real love.

Interior work is demanding, and generally unrewarded externally. The practice of thought control is one of the most important of the spiritual practices, yet is generally unacknowledged. If you can find or develop a small community of seekers with whom to share a commitment to practice, it can be enormously helpful.

Perverted Love

Whereas excessive love is misuse of the human power to desire, and defective love is misuse of the human power to will, perverted love is considered a misuse of the human power of the intellect. Plato's image for these three powers is that of a chariot: the two horses are respectively that of desire and will, and the driver is the intellect. Plato felt that desire and will/anger needed to be carefully reigned in by the mind (the intellect).[11]

As noted earlier in this chapter, the Christian Cappadocian Fathers disagreed with Plato's assessment that the mind was superior to the other qualities that needed to be accepted but kept on a short rein by the mind. The Cappadocians believed every element of human life was blessed in God's creation and thus meant for good purposes, hence there must be positive value to impulses (desire/anger) that could seem to be mainly destructive. Desire was intended to bring people to God, the great Lover. Will/anger was needed to resist unwholesome temptations. And intellect was meant to engage a person ever more fully into the life of God. The goal of spiritual practice was understood as taking a person through three primary steps toward holiness: first, purgation of all that keeps us from God; second, illumination that gives us eyes to see the world as God does; and third, union with the Divine Being. Intellect helps with the second and third steps, in the discovery of the incredible wonder of the Mystery and the growing capacity to participate in God's very life. There are two problem thoughts involving intellect/mind: vainglory and pride.

Vainglory

It may seem a bit odd to say that vainglory involves taking credit for good things, yet that is what it is. Vainglory does the right thing for the wrong reasons, or we might say, a person (or institution) does a good deed, mainly to be admired rather than from sustained compassion. In the desire to be liked or to get attention, one takes full credit for something that God helped cause to be. Vainglory is like the opposite of dejection; instead of putting oneself down, one puts oneself above even God.

In my own life, I like to think I'm a good writer, and I used to be happy to claim credit for the success of my books. Oh, I might share the credit with my publisher, but after all, I was the author. But over the years, a couple of things happened that caused me to think again about the source of success. I realized that some of my books were selling really well, while others were languishing in sales. Eventually it occurred to me that the success of my books did not directly correspond with which ones were my favorites, but seemed rather to be caused by other, subtle factors. I could work very hard on marketing to little avail, whereas other books seemed just to pop off the shelves (or move through the internet). It occurred to me that when my books were selling well, it was likely because God had some reason for wanting those ideas to be spread about. In another instance, my husband and I and two of the monks at our abbey developed what felt like a new idea—a newly revised process that seemed to be very helpful to participants. Once in a while I heard of other places where a similar idea was being used, but I was more than astonished when I attended a national meeting at which the same process was introduced as being originated by someone else! At first, my nose was a bit out of joint, but then I realized that it really mattered very little who got the credit, as long as the process continued to be of real value to people. The glory was God's.

The primary remedy for vainglory is to be watchful of our thoughts, and then to edit, redirect or change our thoughts. It helps to anticipate difficulties rather than react to them. The key is to practice reverence and adoration, returning to prayer. The positive form of vainglory is to give glory to God in all and to practice gratitude.

Pride

Perhaps it seems strange to us that pride is considered the most serious thought, and lust quite low on the list of harmful thoughts. Certainly as our media reports on religious issues, sex is near the top of the problems mentioned. Although all the harmful thoughts are serious, the tradition has always considered pride the most dangerous. Why? Above all, I think, because pride is the belief (conscious or unconscious) that I don't need the Holy, because I myself am perfect. I can control my destiny, and I am the best person to control that of others. Pride is the sin of the proficient, what we might call the sin of the "Pharisees" in the New Testament. Pride is the problem of the self-righteous, who are often persons who have been practicing the spiritual life for many years. Pride involves thoughts of exaggerated self-importance, and causes the collapse of all one's previous spiritual training.

Pride might be thought of as the final madness, supposing we can do anything without God. In a culture suffused with the thought that God is irrelevant, the problem of pride might scarcely cause a ripple on the Richter scale of social convention. It is, in fact, very difficult for anyone in our culture to entirely avoid the sense of God's absence or unimportance. As a result, this listing of troubling thoughts may seem quite odd or unnecessary, because it requires some awareness of the Mystery which surrounds us and some desire to deepen our relationship with that Mystery. Pride brings us back to the beginning of this discussion of the practice of thought control and the development of virtue and personal integrity.

Why This Practice?

This chapter proposes an important spiritual practice of personal integrity or virtue. Integrity means being whole, having that focused attention which early Christians called purity of heart. As we noted, the opposite of virtue is fragmentation, being constantly pulled in many directions, grabbing quickly at the best bang for the buck or the most exciting transitory option, and eventually forgetting altogether those interior standards by which life gains meaning and purpose. All this involves the development of personal character, the capacity to act according to interior values, the vital strength at the core of one's being.

Wholeness or virtue involves both the development of character and also the deepening of relationship with God for the nature of the human is to be incomplete without the love and help of God, carried in our soul as a daily reality. The Christian tradition understands the ultimate form of presence with and to God as something called union, or also participation in God's very being. Our term for this intensity of relationship is not unity, which suggests no distinction between partners, but union, which is an intimate relationship between more than one. God is always Mystery, beyond complete human knowing, even at the stage of union. But in our union with God, humans are able to receive the quality of participation in God that enables us to act with God's will and being in the world. The Christians who report experiencing this union seldom seem *to feel* how blessed they are; indeed apparently the closer we are to God, the more we are blinded by God's glory and brilliance and humbled by our smallness.

The thought practices in this chapter are ones that Christian tradition tells us are specifically designed to strengthen our relationship with God, leading to union. It began with a reference to Jesus's Sermon on the Mount, in which he repeatedly urges a shift from focus on a particular action to a focus on renewal of *how we think*. I have often wondered why some commentators express the view that the Sermon on the Mount is a good ethical system with no necessary connection to a relationship with God. The thought practices recommended in this chapter seem to me to be daunting and difficult, and I cannot imagine that anyone could sustain these practices without God's help. But perhaps no one is likely to try these practices unless they have a desire for that wholeness of being and participation in God which comes both from our own work and from God's help. We are never alone in our desire.

SAMPLE EXERCISES

Self Observation

In this practice we will cultivate the ability to stand a little distance from our thoughts and observe them. We begin by noticing the messages we give ourselves on a regular basis. Dedicate a day or two to this first step in your observations. Keep a piece of paper near you for this exercise. What are your first thoughts upon waking? Do you offer yourself kindness and a gentle welcome to the day, or is your inner voice a snarky drill sergeant telling you to get your lazy self up and out of bed? When you look in the mirror are you compassionate and tender to the self you see there, or do you lament the age, blemishes, and fictional faults you see there? As you move through the day, notice the tone in your mind. Do you dwell in the sense that there is enough time for everything you need to accomplish, or is there a shrill sense that you are always late or somehow insufficient to the task at hand?

After a few days of self-observation, take your reflections to God in prayer. Ask God to give you the eyes to see yourself as God sees you, and to think of yourself with divine graciousness. If you have been harsh with yourself, invite God to help you retrain your thoughts to include kindness and mercy especially towards yourself. You might consider looking at Isaiah 43:4: "You are precious in my sight and honored, and I love you." This is a love letter from God written to you personally. Begin to move into daily practice of self-compassion.

Praying for our Enemies

One essential aspect of learning to observe and amend our thoughts involves bringing everything before God. Jesus was deeply aware of the human tendency to hold grudges, point accusing fingers, and create cultures of hostility. In his Sermon on the Mount, he radically alters the normal trajectory of human behavior inviting us to pray for our enemies (Matthew 5:43). Enemies can be both within and outside of us. What is being invited here is a retraining of the mind and the cultivation of a posture of loving kindness towards all that we perceive as threatening. This practice addresses the challenge of our anger both as it is directed towards others and towards ourselves.

This practice is grounded in a posture of prayer. Find a place where you can be still and uninterrupted for a comfortable period of time. Begin by inviting God to accompany you in this practice. Call to mind someone of whom you are fond. Feel the warm energy in you as you think how grateful you are that this person is in your life, and recognize that God wants their best good to be a reality. See them as a beloved child of God. Now bring to mind someone who is neutral to you, a person whom you neither like nor dislike. Repeat the pattern outlined above. Take time to recognize that God wants their best good to be a reality. See them as a beloved child of God. Finally, call to mind a person with whom you are in conflict, or whom you find disagreeable.

Take time to recognize that God wants their best good to be a reality. Spend a moment softening your own heart towards them and attempt to see them as a beloved child of God. Thank God for placing this person in your life.

FOR FURTHER READING

Allen, Diogenes. *Spiritual Theology*. Boston: Cowley, 1997.

Bouyer, Louis. *A History of Christian Spirituality: Vol I: The Spirituality of the New Testament and the Fathers*. NY: Seabury Press, 1982.

Carter, Stephen L. *Integrity*. New York: Harper/Perseus, 1996.

Cassian, John. *Conferences*. Transl. Colum Luibheid. NY: Paulist, 1985.

Funk, Mary Margaret. *Thoughts Matter: The Practice of the Spiritual Life*. NY: Continuum, 1998.

Hauerwas, Stanley. *The Peaceable Kingdom: A Primer in Christian Ethics*. Notre Dame: IN: University of Notre Dame Press, 1991.

Killinger, Barbara. *Integrity: Doing the Right Thing for the Right Reason*. Montreal: McGill-Queens University Press, 2010.

MacIntyre, Alasdair. *After Virtue*. Notre Dame, IN: University of Notre Dame Press, 2007.

Chapter 8

Social Justice: The Practice of Service

"What we would like to do is change the world—make it a little simpler for people to feed, clothe, and shelter themselves as God intended them to do. And, by fighting for better conditions, by crying out unceasingly for the rights of the workers, the poor, of the destitute—the rights of the worthy and the unworthy poor, in other words—we can, to a certain extent, change the world; we can work for the oasis, the little cell of joy and peace in a harried world. We can throw our pebble in the pond and be confident that its ever widening circle will reach around the world. We repeat, there is nothing we can do but love, and, dear God, please enlarge our hearts to love each other, to love our neighbor, to love our enemy as our friend."

Dorothy Day

Mystery Revealed

Drawing closer to God is a bit like falling in love. As our relationship with the Holy deepens and expands we find ourselves longing for an even greater sense of connection with God, who moves from being an idea to becoming a reality and a tangible presence, and we are drawn into living encounters with the source of the Great Love we have found. As that relationship expands, much like our human relationships, we find ourselves wanting to know more about the Divine One. A holy curiosity begins to emerge centering on questions about God's nature and character. Who is this One who sings to us in the still hours of the night? What does my beloved love? Quick on the heels of those questions is another essential wondering for the spiritual journey, "for what purpose were we created?" What is the essence of the Holy One who calls us to follow, and how can we best serve, love, and cause God joy? These questions are at the heart of the new identity that unfolds as we are drawn closer into the heart of God.

While much of the reality of God is shrouded in mystery, the witness of both the Old Testament, and the person of Jesus in the New Testament are full of revelations of the nature of God. A careful walk through the formative stories of scripture show us what God most loves, celebrates, defends, asks of us, and desires for our well-being, and the well-being of creation. Through the exploration and indwelling of these stories we begin to see who God is, and what God calls us to be and do in the world as God's followers.

Perhaps one of the most powerful Old Testament revelations of God comes from the Exodus story in scripture. Most of us know it as the story in which God calls the Israelites out of slavery into the wilderness and on to the Promised Land, and it is indeed that story. The character of God revealed in that story is of One who actively chooses to liberate the slave and reject the politics of oppression and exploitation of the wealthy and powerful. The second chapter of Exodus tells us that God hears the cries of those who suffer and God actively responds. This radical act of rescue and provision becomes the cornerstone of the identity of God's people and a story that we ourselves are called to enact on behalf of others in gratitude to God. Over and over again throughout all of scripture God says, "I did it for you, you do it for them." Thus, some of the most essential and primary spiritual practices that connect us to God are service to others, and working for justice, peace, and reconciliation in the world.

God's Calling Card

In a world that is often consumed with resumes and titles, it is illuminating to see how God chooses to be identified. As Moses is about to lead the Israelites into the Promised Land he warns them not to forget God's graciousness to them in their many years of wandering in the wilderness. Moses summarizes the law for the people one more time and then reminds them of God's credentials,

"For The Lord your God is God of gods and Lord of lords, the great God, mighty and awesome, who is not partial and takes no bribe, who executes justice for the orphan and the widow, and who loves the strangers, providing them food and clothing. You shall also love the stranger, for you were strangers in the land of Egypt. You shall fear the Lord your God; him alone you shall worship." (Deuteronomy 10:17-20)

God's calling card is care for the widows and orphans. God's resume is compassion and care for the stranger. Even though this passage says God is not partial, we see that God is indeed partial to the widows, orphans, and homeless strangers, and God calls us to imitate that same active care and provision for the fragile around us. This introduction and listing of the compassionate aspect of God is repeated again and again throughout scripture. Psalm 68 identifies God as "The father of orphans and protector of widows is God in his holy habitation. God gives the desolate a home to live in; he leads the prisoners to prosperity" (verses 5-6). There is no mistaking that God is the champion of the weak and is actively engaged in caring for the poor. As God's people we are invited and challenged to do the same. God calls us to "pay it forward" in love and gratitude.

A window on God's call to remember our own humble and fragile origins and God's astonishing mercy emerges for me in a story from my teenage years. It was a number of years ago that I took my parents' car out to go to the movies with friends. The details of the original incident are shrouded in memory, but somehow the car did not come home in the same condition it had left the safety of their garage. A couple thousand dollars of damage had been done in a parking lot fender bender and I was responsible. My parents let me work off the debt, about fifty dollars a month, using a portion of my earnings at my part time waitressing job. Month after month I subtracted the numbers, and still it seemed like I was getting nowhere. Even after a year, I still owed over a thousand dollars. That debt was going to be with me a long, long time. It hung over me like a dark cloud. Graduation from high school came and my parent's handed me an envelope. In it was a card of congratulations and a note telling me that my debt had been cancelled. I was so happy I cried. A huge burden had been lifted and I was free, forgiven even. Somehow I remember asking how I could ever repay them, and their answer was even more grace filled. "Someday do this for your own kids, or if you see somebody whose load is heavier than they can lift, help them out."

Grounded in Gratitude

This is the heart of what God speaks to each of us when we begin to comprehend the amazing grace with which each of us is loved and forgiven. As grace and gratitude begin to take over our lives we are filled with a love for God that requires enacting. The challenge with showing gratitude to God is that we cannot actually hug God, return the favor, or give anything to the One who literally has it all. So what does God answer when we ask, "How can I repay you for all the goodness you have shown me?" That question prompts the writing of a foundational passage from the prophet Micah. Micah wonders aloud if God wants burnt offerings, or livestock, or oil, or the gift of his first born child in gratitude for all that God has given him, and then Micah remembers what God really truly desires, "He has told you, O mortal, what is good; and what does the Lord require of you but to do justice, and to love kindness, and to walk humbly with your God?" (Micah 6:6-8)

Not as Easy as It Sounds

It sounds so simple. Like a three-step recipe, but these commands alone are a lifetime's spiritual work. Once we reach the Promised Land, or become aware that our debt is forgiven we often don't really want to remember how bad it was, and encountering the suffering of others is difficult and painful. While we are deeply grateful to God for the gifts we have been given, rather than go looking for someone else who needs to be blessed, it seems easier to sing songs, or write prayers, or have festivals celebrating God's goodness than it is to rescue the orphan and care for the widow. This is nothing new. God's people have seemingly long had a bit of a problem with active personal caring. The prophet Isaiah gives voice to God's frustration with the priests' and people's multitude of sacrifices and festivals. God was tired of the liturgical pageant that seemed to be far more about show and far less about actually loving our neighbor.

> "What to me is the multitude of your sacrifices? . . . I have had enough of burnt offerings of rams and the fat of fed beasts; . . . Wash yourselves; make yourselves clean; remove the evil of your doings from before my eyes; cease to do evil, learn to do good; seek justice, rescue the oppressed, defend the orphan, plead for the widow." (Isaiah 1:1-18)

The full power of this text came alive for me after I had been
ordained to the ministry for several years and was serving in the Spiritual Formation Program at Columbia Theological Seminary in Decatur,
Georgia. My husband and I were raising two little kids and worship-
ping at Central Presbyterian Church in downtown Atlanta, a congregation deeply grounded in outreach and advocacy for the poor. The
church ran a homeless shelter in the winter months and some eighty-
five men were housed and fed in the gym connected to the church.
There were a number of doctors in the congregation who noticed that
the men's feet were in particularly bad shape. We learned that if you
live and sleep on the street, you don't dare take off your shoes when
you sleep, because when you wake up your shoes will not be there.
You also don't get many chances to bathe and wash your feet, and you
may walk many miles between rest stops. Seeing all this, the doctors
opened up a foot clinic. They taught volunteers to offer shelter guests
a warm foot soak, a very simple pedicure to trim overgrown toenails
and care for callouses, a quick massage with some Vicks VapoRub, and
fresh socks for anyone who wanted them.

Each Sunday of shelter season the call went out to the congregation that more volunteers were needed for this hands-on ministry.
Each Sunday I pretended that the invitation was not for me, I was far
too busy chasing toddlers and doing important liturgical and educa-
tional things to make time for this. This dodging of God's call worked
well until I took a walk in the neighborhood among the many faculty
houses of the seminary professors. I happened to run into a friend who
was also a church member, a mom of teenage girls, and one of the New
Testament professors. When I asked her what she was doing that night
she told me she and the girls, yes, her twelve and fourteen year olds,
were going to volunteer at the foot clinic and asked if I would like to
come along. I was completely stuck, delightfully so. God had jumped
my last wall with a personal invitation. If this amazing woman and
her kids could enact their love for God in such a personal way, then I
simply had to try.

It was not easy or comfortable, but it was holy. Seeing and tending
to the broken feet of some of God's children made the love of God real
to me in a way that defies description. An astonishing sense of unity
and compassion emerged in me. Any previously held construct of "us
and them" was literally washed away at the foot clinic. There was a
pervading sense of worship far deeper than most church services I
had led or attended as we poured the water and massaged tired feet.

There was gentle laughter and the tumbling of barriers as socks were tugged on tired, freshly-washed feet. God was present in that tiny hallway of folding chairs, and my heart knew that this kind of loving care was indeed what God desired. Hands on, personal and active caring mattered at least as much, if not more, to God than all my words and prayers. This was a new way to tell and show God of my love, and in God's astonishing way, it became a way in which I was also able to receive that love as well.

A Model to Follow

In addition to the joy and mutual blessing I found in the work at the foot clinic, what I most remember is the gift of my friend's invitation. Rather than assume I had better things to do, or that I wouldn't want to join her, she echoed Jesus's call to "come and see" (John 1:39). She offered me a model to follow. More than that, she followed up her invitation with personal accompaniment and even a ride to the church that evening. She became a door through which I could participate in the joyful work of the kingdom of God.

Though there are numerous theological treatises written on the person and the work of Christ, undoubtedly one essential aspect of Christ's mission here on earth was to actually show us what it looks like when one takes God's command to love our neighbor as ourselves as the essence of our life's work. In Christ, God both invites and illustrates how to come and follow this life-changing path of enacting gratitude through loving service to others. Just as God's identity, nature, and summons to us is care for the fragile, so too we find Christ standing in the synagogue and reading from the ancient text of Isaiah announcing,

> "The Spirit of The Lord is upon me, because he has anointed me to bring good news to the poor. He has sent me to proclaim release to the captives and recovery of sight to the blind, to let the oppressed go free, and to proclaim the year of the Lord's favor" (Luke 4:18).

Later in John's Gospel Jesus will tell the disciples that in seeing him, they have seen the Father. The loving mercy that they witness in the actions and teaching of Jesus are not just echoes of God, but also the incarnation of God's intention to do justice and love kindness.

To begin with, Jesus doesn't choose the rabbis or other powerful people of the day to accompany him in his ministry. He chooses simple people. From there he goes to the places that all the religious authorities deeply believed made one unclean, or at the very least were unseemly in which to be seen. In Mark and Luke's gospels Jesus's first healing act is the cleansing of a leper. Levitical law has exiled these people for generations, but Jesus responds in tenderness when approached by this outcast (Luke 5:12-16. Mark 1:40). In Matthew's gospel, Jesus's first act of ministry is to preach compassion to all who are suffering, encouragement to those who are disheartened, and then to reinterpret the law so that it becomes astonishingly grace filled (Matthew 5). Advocating for the dignity and value of women, Jesus radically alters the tradition of casual divorce of casting women aside for any reason at all by harnessing it with a serious consequence for men. He declares retaliation and violence a thing of the past, and charges his followers to, "give to anyone who begs from you, and do not refuse anyone who wants to borrow from you" (Matthew 5:42). Any single one of these ideas is ridiculous enough, but the sum of them together is nearly incomprehensible for hearers of his day. Even to us who are familiar with his teachings, a slow prayerful listening to his words can invoke some profound ethical and spiritual discomfort. Jesus exhibits the love and justice of God as he is drawn into the places where people need encouragement and healing, and as he daringly challenges the current cultural, religious, and political system where it is broken and damaging. We admire him, we bless him, we celebrate his courage, but what he asks for is for us to come and do likewise. The blessing woven in that invitation is that not only are we shown the path of practicing service in love, but by the grace of the Holy Spirit we are given all that we need in order to actually walk it. Just as my friend made the invitation and then provided the way, so Christ accompanies us in this work. The challenge in following him will be in wrestling with our self-image, and doubts as they arise along the way.

Resisting the Invitation

Gerald May offers us an extremely helpful window into the internal conflict we encounter as we both fall more deeply in love with God, and find our defenses of self-preservation arising as we encounter God's call and claim on our lives. May writes eloquently about the deep human desire and longing for what he calls a unitive experience of God, referring to an experience of the Holy in which, if even just for a moment, the self is lost.[1] This is the kind of spontaneous awe-filled moment that is a central desire of many spiritual practices. What May points out so well is that even as we so deeply desire this kind of unitive experience, our egos, that part of ourselves by which we create an identity to present to the world, fight such a holy encounter because we know it means loss and change in the way we understand ourselves and our place in the world. Back and forth we wrestle, drawing near and running away from God. We get close and no sooner are we near the threshold of the holy than we turn and run the other direction.

This dynamic is perfectly portrayed in the story of the rich young man who comes to ask Jesus what good deeds he must do to inherit eternal life (Matthew 19:16-22). Jesus redirects the young man's attention to the goodness of God, and reminds him to keep the commandments. The young man assures Jesus that he has already done that, but wonders if there is anything else he must do. Jesus tells him that if he wishes to be perfect he will need to go and sell all his possessions, and give the money to the poor and then come and follow Christ. This instruction is simply too much. The cost of following Jesus and sacrificing his belongings is more than the young man can bear and he walks away in despair. We join him in that tension of knowing that our identity will be radically altered if we actually follow the example and invitation of Jesus in self–sacrifice and service. We can't help but wrestle with letting go and surrendering into the radical trust that is required in the practice of service. It is not comfortable, and it flies in the face of the cultural narrative that tells us that we are to climb the ladder of success, not descend in personal sacrifice. Again, the great gift is that we are called to do this with God's promise to accompany and empower us for this work. Our job is to choose to say yes, and allow God to lead the way.

Pause for reflection:
- *Take a moment and consider the story above. Are there possessions getting in the way of your willingness and availability to follow God? What would it be like to begin by reducing your possessions by some portion, perhaps ten percent? There are numerous agencies in most communities that welcome donations of household goods, clothes, and furniture. What can you clear out to make space for God, and to share with the poor?*

Redefining Holiness

Taking on the role of a servant, associating with classes of people that we deem lower than ourselves, giving away time and money, risking our standing and even safety in community by challenging the authorities— none of this has ever been easy or comfortable for humans. Even the disciples, who had witnessed the miracles and heard every teaching first hand, still argued about who was going to be the greatest (Matthew 18:1-5). The religious leaders of Jesus's time also had a tough time with Jesus's expansive love and benevolent interpretation of scripture. In one of the early tests that they put to Jesus, he manages to take the opportunity to further broaden the definitions of holiness and community. In yet another story one of the lawyers asks Jesus the same question as the rich young man, that is, "What must I do to inherit eternal life?" (Luke 10:25). Jesus offers the man a chance to show his knowledge of the law and they both agree that what God asks is to *"Love the Lord your God with all your heart, and with all your soul, and with all your strength, and with all your mind, and your neighbor as yourself"* (Luke 10:27).

But the lawyer will not let it go. Once again, we see the impulse of self-preservation, the desire to pick a fight, and perhaps the need to discredit Jesus make him push the issue. "But who is my neighbor?" he asks. This question gives Jesus the opportunity once again to show just how outrageously large God's vision of mercy and justice are. Jesus answers by telling the story of the Good Samaritan. It is a story that both humiliates the religious elite and celebrates the racial ethnic outcast. In the story a man is robbed and beaten and left for dead on the side of the road. Both the priest and the Levite, each one a religious functionary, ignore the man and his suffering and pass by on the opposite side of the road. The hero of the story is a Samaritan, a culturally reviled person in the context in which Jesus is preaching. The Samaritan stops his own journey, bandages the wounded man, and transports him to an inn for further care, all at his own expense. Just to be sure those gathered to hear the story get his point Jesus then asks the lawyer a question: "Which one of these three, do you think, was a neighbor to the man who fell into the hands of the robbers?" There is no doubt in anyone's mind what the correct answer is, and the lawyer responds, "The one who showed mercy." In affirmation and command Jesus replies, to all of us willing to hear, "Go and do likewise." Rather than limit the definition of the neighbor whom we are to love as we love ourselves, Jesus expands the pool and charges all of us to show mercy each and every chance we get. And just in case we have any doubt at all about what Jesus is asking of us, he tells yet another story which redefines our *eternal* identities based on how we responded to others in need.

In perhaps one of the more unsettling stories that he tells about his desire for us to care for the most vulnerable, Jesus shares a story about judgment of the nations. What is disturbing to many is that no mention of confession of faith is made. Jesus says that all people will be gathered before the throne of God and then separated out just as a shepherd separates sheep from goats. One of the groups is to be blessed, and the other cursed. The group that is to be blessed are the ones who fed Jesus when he was hungry, offered him a drink when he was thirsty, welcomed him when he was a stranger, clothed him when he was naked, took care of him when he was sick, and visited him in prison. This makes absolutely no sense to them since they say they never saw him in any of these situations. Likewise, those to be cursed are being punished for not caring for Jesus when he most needed it. Curiously, they too say they never saw him in need. Jesus reveals his identification and solidarity with all those who suffer when he tells them their care, or lack thereof, for the "least of these" was done "unto him" (Matthew 25:31-46). How we practice caring for the least of these is how we practice caring and showing our love for Christ. The way we are in relationship with all others is the way we are in relationship with God. Now that we have clarity about the importance of this practice, let us consider the practicalities of how to begin on a personal level.

Charity and Justice

At worship in a nearby Catholic church recently, a young boy stood and thanked the congregation for its hard work and generosity in donating so much food to the food pantry. After he spoke, an older man stood and challenged the people gathered to join him in writing letters to the state and federal representatives encouraging them to enact legislation that would alleviate the sources of hunger and poverty. These two faces offer for us a glimpse of two streams of compassion in which Jesus calls us to participate. They also offer us a lovely image for the distinction between charity and advocacy for justice. Charity is a gift from our abundance by which we see and respond to the needs of those around us. Justice is somewhat trickier to try to define.

What Exactly Does It Mean to Do Justice?

We tend to toss around the word *justice* somewhat casually at times, and most of us imagine that we know what it is. As a young seminarian I was certain I knew what justice was and that I wanted to participate in causes that were just. It was just such a remark that launched one of my professors into a passionate declaration that, "You young people have no idea what justice is! Justice, justice, you cry, but you don't know what you are asking. When you say you want justice you are asking that every hurtful, cruel, selfish thing you have ever said or done in your life be perpetrated back on you. That would be justice!" Not one of us could breathe or move when he finished speaking. The truth of what he said was deeply convicting. His comments also illuminated the difference between different types of justice. What he was speaking about was retributive justice where the punishment is completely parallel to the crime, as in an eye for an eye.

The type of justice that we want to explore here is what is known as social justice in which we wrestle with how best to set up institutions and communities in which each person can lead a fulfilling life and contribute to community no matter what their circumstances might be. Thus we find there is a personal component to following Christ, the way of charity and service, and a corporate and political component which is actively working in the world and challenging the systems which perpetuate inequalities and oppression. In many of the world's societies the systems by which the workers receive a fair wage, the homeless are housed, and the sick are tended are all based in the sphere of governmental policies. We are charged to be informed advocates on behalf of those whose voice is minimized in the structures of power.

How Do We Begin?

The first movement of this practice is a willingness to see the need that surrounds us on a daily basis. We are invited to see poverty outside ourselves as well as our own personal poverty of spirit, and perhaps even poverty of faith. Each one of us is both rich and poor in many ways. We begin the practice of service by acknowledging our own needs, failures, longings, and hunger for God, and we claim God's sufficiency. "My grace is sufficient, for my power is made perfect in your weakness" (2 Cor. 12:9). From this place of encouraged humility we can begin to ask God to open our eyes and hearts to others.

This is a painful and vulnerable first step. Many of us fear that we will be overwhelmed if we open our hearts to the needs of others. Choosing to be willing to be broken open in compassion is the beginning of a holy transformation. As we allow God to show us the pain of the world, we also deepen our trust in God who desires that the world be made whole, and who holds the power to make it so. Each of us is already aware of many of the needs in our community and our world. The first step is to be willing to see it with the eyes of God's love.

The next step is simply to agree to try to serve in whatever small way we can. Some people have the gift of being able to jump right in and respond. One of my dear friends saw the devastation in Haiti on television after the most recent earthquake and knew she had to book a flight and simply go. Others of us need to take smaller steps on this journey. God seems ready to offer the accommodations we need if we simply ask. There are agencies, ministries, service groups, and leaders in caring work in every community. Each community has a system of care through which it responds to those in need. Learn about your community's system of care and be willing to find your place in it. Every school needs extra helpers with reading and other projects. Nursing homes need volunteers to help with activities. Soup kitchens need meal preparers. No act of caring is ever too trivial or too small. Listen for the invitation of the Spirit and allow yourself to be led out of your comfort zone. Beginning steps in living into this practice can be as simple as checking in on an elderly neighbor, or donating food to your local food bank. Those who work and live in urban settings might consider a spiritual practice of carrying extra transit tokens and water to give to those in need as they move through the city. What is called for in this practice is summed up in the prayer one of my friends shared with me, "Lord, let me see what you see, help me love what you love, and if you have work or service for me to do today, help me not to avoid your call."

Practicalities and Pitfalls of this Practice

One of the greatest challenges of this practice is not succumbing to despair. Once we open our eyes and hearts to see and respond to the suffering in the world it can seem as if that is all there is around us. The swamp of sorrow and feelings of futility expand before us when we lose sight of God who is the director and initiator of our caring. We can get incredibly discouraged if we begin to think that redemption and the transformation of suffering is up to us. Attempting to launch out on our own crusade, or expecting monumental changes in reality are a recipe for frustration. We are called above all to show mercy, love kindness, and walk humbly with God who is the initiator and sustainer of all of our plans for helping. To quote the literature of Stephen Ministries, "We care, God cures."[2]

One of the first steps is caring, showing mercy, and responding to the many needs around us by actually entering into relationship and listening to those whom we hope to care for. In my work with the homeless, when I ask what is the most difficult part of their lives they often say, "not being seen as human," or "having people not look at you at all." This prompted a first step practice for me of seeing and greeting anyone I met on the street as though they were a friend. Often it is followed with a request for money. One of my teachers in this practice encouraged me to invite those who are asking for money on the street to join me for a meal or a cup of coffee and thus humanize the encounter. On the few occasions that I have had the presence, time, and grace to do so, I have been deeply blessed. Conversation can be daunting at first, but simple questions about where the person grew up, what he or she liked to do as a kid, and if he or she is familiar with the services available in the community can fill that void. A good closing to the visit might be to ask how you could be praying for them. You might also ask them to pray for you as well. In that way we acknowledge our mutual brokenness, and the gift that we can be to one another. Great care must be taken as we reach out in service not to exacerbate the poverty of the economically poor. An internal posture of mutuality and regard for others must be cultivated so that we do not add to the shame, dependence, and sense of inferiority of those who are already struggling. We must urgently resist the unintentional use of the poor as objects to create a sense of accomplishment or personal righteousness.

It is also important not to assume that we know the needs of others when we encounter them in suffering. The poor are all too often victims of our well-intentioned efforts. On a service trip in Mexico we worked with an agency to build a classroom that would expand service in that rural area. As we worked, one of our team noticed an air conditioner in the window of the main building and commented that it might be great to take a break in there since the heat was sweltering. Our guide laughed and said that was a classic example of sending a gift that no one could use. She said a well-meaning group from the U.S. had sent that unit down to her school to help the children learn in comfort, but never checked to see that there was electricity in the building (there wasn't). So there it sits, a monument to solving problems without being in relationship or asking questions.

Perhaps one of the most provocative books on this topic, *When Helping Hurts: How to Alleviate Poverty without Hurting the Poor . . . And Yourself*, by Steve Corbett and Brian Fikkert challenges our notion of what the goal of service might be.

> The goal is not to make the materially poor all over the world, into middle-to-upper-class North Americans. . . . Rather, the goal is to restore people to a full expression of humanness, to being what God created us all to be, people who glorify God by living in right relationship with God, with self, with others, and with the rest of creation.[3]

We begin this restoration of right relationship within ourselves, and from a place of grounded compassion we reach out in love and service to others.

Yet another important aspect of this practice has to be the willingness to release the outcome. Jesus tells a parable in Matthew's gospel about weeds among the wheat. While there are varying interpretations of this story, the final word is that God is the one who will take care of the results in the end (Matthew 13:24-30). We often don't get to see the fruits of our labors, but are called to serve anyway. Maybe one more person will know God's love through our actions. Maybe we ourselves will encounter grace and mercy in a fresh way by being vulnerable and available. We cannot be guided or hindered by the false deities of success or failure, only love. That is not to say we do not attempt to offer the best care possible, but rather that we trust that God will take our offering and do as God wishes with it. Perhaps one of the best known servants of this century, Mother Teresa, modified a powerful set of paradoxical commandments by author Dr. Kent M. Keith, when she said,

> People are unreasonable, illogical, and self-centered. Love them anyway. If you do good, people may accuse you of selfish motives. Do good anyway. If you are successful, you may win false friends and true enemies. Succeed anyway. The good you do today may be forgotten tomorrow. Do good anyway. Honesty and transparency make you vulnerable. Be honest and transparent anyway. What you spend years building may be destroyed overnight. Build anyway. People who really want help may attack you if you help them. Help them anyway. Give the world the best you have and you may get hurt. Give the world your best anyway.[4]

SAMPLE EXERCISES

Let Your Heart Lead You

What situation in the world are you most passionate about? What tugs at your heart when you hear about it? Are you moved by hunger in the world? Do you wish the world were safer for children? When you see the homeless in your community do you wish there was a solution? Do racial or gender inequalities concern you? Each of us has been given a gift for the building up of the community, and we can often find God's invitation woven into our discontent. Make a list of all the causes that feel compelling to you. Decide to choose one problem in the world that you will actively and personally respond to in service. Begin to research agencies that respond to the need with which you feel a sense of kinship. Set a deadline for getting involved. If you are feeling awkward about starting, gather a friend or two and begin together. If you need a smaller window perhaps you might choose the liturgical season of Lent or Advent in which to actively care and advocate for others.

Read, Pray, Do

This exercise invites participants to read the newspaper with an eye to God's call to service. If you are not a newspaper subscriber there are many online news sources available at no cost. Begin in prayer by asking to be given God's eyes with which to see the stories. Read with compassion. See with mercy. Look for the victims, and wonder about where the widows and orphans are in these stories. Who needs prayer in the story you are reading? Both the oppressor and oppressed are precious to God, and both are in need of prayer. Commit to reading the paper in this way each day for at least two weeks. Is there a call to action emerging as you read?

One Act a Day that is Not for You

The purpose of this exercise is to help us get beyond ourselves, and begin to be aware of and responsive to the needs of others. Choose a week in which each day you will seek to do an act of kindness or service that is not for you and will not benefit you or your family in any way. It can be anonymous, or you may find yourself in relationship with the recipient of your service such as mowing the lawn of an elderly neighbor or volunteering at a soup kitchen. You can plan these out in advance or look for opportunities to show God's love in a spontaneous way. Notice how much of your day is spent paying attention to your own needs. Notice how it feels to care for others. Pay attention to your sense of God's presence as you look outward on behalf of others.

Take a prayer walk or drive in your community

Rather than turn away from poverty, hunger, and need simply allow yourself to be present on behalf of God. Choose to walk or drive through a part of your community that may be unfamiliar to you. Begin by praying to see with God's eyes. What might God's prayer be for the people you encounter? Can you be a blessing simply by praying your way through this part of your community? Notice when you begin to move toward judgment and resist that movement. When you return home take some time to journal about what you saw and felt as you walked.

FOR FURTHER READING

Boesak, Allan Aubrey and Curtiss Paul DeYoung. *Radical Reconciliation: Beyond Political Pietism and Christian Quietism.* Maryknoll, NY: Orbis Books, 2014.

Brueggemann, Walter. *The Prophetic Imagination.* Philadelphia: Fortress Press, 1978.

Claiborne, Shane. *The Irresistible Revolution.* Michigan: Zondervan, 2006

Corbett, Steve and Fikkert, Brian. *When Helping Hurts: How to Alleviate Poverty Without Hurting the Poor . . . And Yourself.* Chicago: Moody Publishers, 2009.

Day, Keri. *Unfinished Business: Black Women, the Black Church, and the Struggle to Thrive in America.* Maryknoll, NY: Orbis Books, 2014.

Keller, Timothy. *Generous Justice.* New York: Penguin Group, 2010.

Labberton, Mark. *The Dangerous Act of Loving Your Neighbor: Seeing Others Through the Eyes of Jesus.* Illinois: InterVarsity Press, 2010.

McDuff, Mallory. *Natural Saints: How People of Faith are Working to Save God's Earth.* New York: Oxford University Press, 2013.

Patel, Eboo. *Sacred Ground: Pluralism, Prejudice, and the Promise of America.* Boston: Beacon Press, 2012.

Wallis, Jim. *The (Un)Common Good: How the Gospel brings Hope to a World Divided.* Grand Rapids, MI: Brazos Press, 2014.

Chapter 9

Uncertainty and Change: The Practice of Resilience

We have said farewell to much of Newtonian physics
and stand now in a quantum world-view, which gives us
greater appreciation of the role of chaos in creation.
(Our task now) is to leave those who can surf the seeming chaos to do so
without restrictions and with maximum trust.

Sr. Ishpriya (in *The Way*, October 1995)

Stability and Disorientation

Jesus was fond of unsettling people. We may prefer to think of him as bringing comfort to people, and indeed, he did that. Yet we may have become so accustomed to his teachings, or so remote from his world and that of his immediate hearers, that we no longer notice how very unsettling his words often were. To carefully observant religious minds, he breaks the solemnity of the Sabbath by healing (Luke 6:6-11) and by feeding his hungry disciples (Mark 2:23-28). To Peter's passionate claim that Jesus is too important to be killed, Jesus responds by calling Peter "Satan" (Matt. 16:21-23). Many of Jesus's parables seem intended to confuse his listeners of the time: mustard seeds created weeds that often overwhelmed the "good crops," and leaven was thought of as an impure mold, from which a home needed regularly to be cleansed. How could such "invaders" be considered symbols of the kingdom of God? (Matt 13:31-3). Such teachings disrupt the ordered life and invite us to consider a God most unlike our expectations, one whose gift of *confusion is somehow meant to be life-giving*. This sort of unsettling advice is not limited to Jesus; we find similar examples from teachers in many religions.

Why should it be part of a spiritual teaching that things be unsettled? Or, perhaps more directly relevant to our practice, are uncertainty and change important to spiritual growth? Much as we might prefer not to hear it, the answer is a resounding Yes! Although uncertainty and change almost inevitably create anxiety, there is every evidence that they are necessary in spiritual formation for the simple reason that human nature tends to grow comfortable and static unless unexpected and unsettling things happen occasionally.

Stability and Conversion

Because of my years studying Benedictine spirituality, I find the Benedictine vows a useful way to consider the matter of change in the spiritual life. Many people think that religious vows are poverty, chastity, and obedience. Actually, the vow that Benedictine monastics make is to stability, obedience, and a peculiar thing called *conversatio morum suorum*. The Latin phrase doesn't make much sense, so sometimes this third part of the single vow is simply translated, "the monastic way of life," but that translation is not particularly useful for those of us living in the world. So I prefer the translation "daily conversion of heart," or more simply "conversion." Benedict asks that we commit ourselves both to stability and to daily conversion of heart.[1]

Stability

Both stability and conversion are foundational to the spiritual life, in whatever form we live them. For monastics, stability means a commitment to a specific place and a specific community for the rest of their lives. For the common life, it may mean commitment to certain relationships; in today's world, it is unlikely to mean commitment to a workplace and/or a geographic place, due to matters often out of the individual's control. But more specifically, stability refers to an overall sense of being grounded. Simple things like regularity in brushing teeth, eating meals, and daily routines create physical stability. The practice of integrity outlined in chapter 6 can help create emotional stability. And spiritual stability is needed too—a deeply felt conviction that the world is divinely inspirited and that I personally am enfolded in this Spirit. Such spiritual stability may be experienced as a sudden divine intrusion, but more generally it emerges over time and with practice. Monastic stability is founded in this fundamental idea of trust in a reliable God.

How might such trust develop? Sometimes when we feel the touch of God, we discount it, saying "Oh, I just imagined that." An authentic experience of the Holy will, of course, help make us better persons, and generally correspond to the outlines of the tradition we espouse. However, usually the touch of God is not of the sort that can be tested physically or rationally, because the Divine communicates at a different level of experience, via something we might call a true but elusive, imaginal realm.[2] To offer an example from my own life, I was with a group of pilgrims in north Wales when we took a side trip to the island of Anglesey. We had been told that we would visit the holy site of a long ago hermit named Seiriol, located at a natural well. The story was that once a year in the early Celtic period Seiriol would walk west across half the width of Anglesey to meet another hermit walking from the east, meeting at a mid-point. One was called "the red" because he always walked face to the sun, and the other called "the pale" because he always walked with the sun behind him. Something about that simple story captured my imagination, and my heart was hungry, so I made a decision to ask for Seiriol's blessing. After the others in the group had gone off to the nearby priory, I stayed behind and knelt at the edge of the well. I asked for guidance, hoping I suppose, for a specific bit of advice. Suddenly I felt quite sure Seiriol was standing behind me, lifting his hands above my head in blessing. And I felt that I heard these words, "Be what you are: Loved, a channel of light." I cannot convey the sense of grace as I stayed there for a few more moments and then rejoined the group. I could hardly speak, and certainly not chitchat, so at our next stop, feeling as if I were walking on air, I went off again by myself to allow the experience to deepen in me for a few more precious moments. (I have since begun to wonder if this pause to deeply absorb a grace is central to spiritual practice.)

What had happened? Perhaps "nothing;" perhaps "something." Yet I was left with a feeling of keen certainty that I had been touched by God, a feeling that has not left me to this day. It is not the only such experience given me, but it is one that I bring back to memory at times to remind myself of the care and wonder of God. Monastic stability is at heart a spiritual stability, growing over time as a deeply felt conviction that the world is filled with a Holy Being who surprisingly and wonderfully cares about me. Spiritual stability finds its roots in trust in a reliable God.

Now a mysterious God is not reliable in the ordinary sense. A profound relationship with God will challenge us in many ways, which is where daily conversion comes in. Yet after time, and/or after experiencing the overwhelming touch of God, our trust grows in God's fidelity to us. As we are faithful to some of the practices discussed in this book, our sense deepens of living in intimate relation to God and assurance of God's life growing in us.

Daily Conversion of Heart

A heart-felt confidence in God is necessary to negotiate the upheavals inevitable in spiritual growth. That's why stability is the necessary partner of ongoing conversion. But ongoing conversion is also necessary. Indeed, God's very self will initiate or allow upheavals and challenges to our faith. As C. S. Lewis observes, "God is the great iconoclast,"[3] the great destroyer of images. Lewis is reflecting after the death of his wife, realizing that what he misses most about Joy is the fact that whenever she was with him, she reminded him that in her absence, he had been tempted to make an "icon" of her, defining her too narrowly in his mind, as if she were a fixed thing. But in her presence, he realized she was vital, alive, slippery, growing, elusive—not a thing but a person in all her complexity. I think this is an apt description of what spiritual people can be tempted to do when thinking of the Holy. Whenever we are not actively aware of God's presence, we tend to think of God as a fixed, knowable quality. But when we are truly present to the Divine, we are spun in the play of *metanoia*, of conversion of heart, so that not only God but we become livelier than we thought. Our images of the Holy and our relationship with the Divine need to be "open stories," open to unfolding possibilities that may bring anxiety because unfamiliar and even challenging to cherished beliefs.

Doubt can be a sign of wondering, eventually strengthening faith. Observers of growth patterns in children consistently point out that movement toward new stages of growth happens when one way of thinking and acting becomes inadequate to account for incoming experiences, a period of vulnerability ensues, and gradually a more expansive stage of awareness emerges.

Faith and Doubt

The father of a boy subject to seizures asks Jesus for help. Jesus says that all things can be done for one who believes. The father cries out, 'I believe; help my unbelief!' (Mark 9:22-29).

We are told that we must have faith, and we take this to mean that we must not doubt. The most well-known doubter in the New Testament is the disciple Thomas, who first queries Jesus's statement that where he goes, he is preparing a place for the disciples. Thomas also is bold enough to tell the other disciples that he will not believe in Jesus's resurrection until he sees and touches the evidence of Jesus's death in the resurrected body (John 14:1-7; John 20:24-29). We often take these passages as evidence that doubt is bad and the opposite of faith. But it is important to note that Thomas is called "The Twin," presumably meaning the twin of Jesus himself, because he was so like Jesus. And Jesus's response to Thomas in both cases is to acknowledge that Thomas (and the boy's father) are asking *to be in relationship* with him. He both honors the requests and says, in effect, "You know me," and that is sufficient.

In our desire for certainty, we are tempted to take Jesus's answer as meaning Jesus is the *only* way to relationship with God. But I think Jesus means something quite different. The fact of God is always wrapped in ambiguity, uncertainty, mystery. The reality of relationship is always dynamic. Jesus does not give Thomas a map to the place he prepares; instead he gives himself, a guide.

To be human is to want control, to *know* what's ahead, to seek certainty. But faith means belief in something unseen, something beyond our ken. It is taking a leap into the unknown, because we have confidence in our companion, our guide. Sometimes we think faith means certainty; but that is exactly what faith does *not* mean. Faith is not possession of the Truth; it is instead being dependent upon the One who is Truth, a Truth that is always expanding out beyond our grasp, a Truth that enlarges our hearts.

Faith is always needing what I myself cannot supply, always being restless outside relationship with Mystery. Faith consents to depend upon the sacramental, the inner grace concealed yet embodied in outer signs. Thomas models clearly what all the disciples felt at certain points, wanting to believe, but troubled and questioning. Even after the resurrection, they "disbelieved for joy and wondered" (Luke 24:41).

Jesus's mother Mary shows us the essential relationship between faith and doubt as she wondered, pondered, and allowed questions to rise in her heart at the ambiguities arising in Jesus's early life (Luke 2:19 and 51). In such a way, we too are invited to respond to the relationship offered by Christ: to engage with our questions, to be persistent and expectant, to wait. Such "doubt" does not descend to the cynical, but is partnered by hope. In such questioning, we become vulnerable to the Other, allowing the relationship to change us.

Faith is not something we have; it is something that has us. Faith is being the person we are—someone in relationship with God in Christ.

Not only does this pattern happen in the growth of children, but it is characteristic of good psychotherapy, and for that matter, good drama. Walter Brueggemann observes that the Psalms reveal a similar pattern of movement from orientation to disorientation to re-orientation, and that so often pain is the matrix of newness.[4] After the Nicene Council prohibited Christians from praying to Jesus as a man, requiring instead that prayers be offered to "Christ" as God-man, a heart rending cry came to us from one of the desert monks. The monk exclaimed, "They have taken away my God and I do not know where to find him!" Such cries, painful as they are, can be the stimulus for an expansion of spiritual awareness, if undertaken willingly.

Spiritual guide Carolyn Gratton has observed that un-asked-for change or necessary losses are the primary concrete opportunities for discovering and unfolding the unique spirit in each of us.[5] Jolts from real life can move us to listen to reality *as it is*, rather than as we would have it be. It takes courage and strength to accept such challenges as the opportunities they are. She is assuring that such opportunities are not tricks but promises.

As Christians we may discover that unwelcome or unsought changes are times to live more deeply into our baptism: metaphorically in our distress we are dying with Christ that we may emerge with him into a resurrected or revitalized form of life. We can re-experience God's commitment to suffer all pain with us, and believe in the possibility of something better ahead than we now see. This is *the practice of resilience*: we bend with the "assaults" of life, rather than rigidly hold on until they break us. Yet, letting go of the structures which have previously enabled us to make sense of the world is risky and painful. To accept the challenge of change can well mean a difficult period ahead, bringing a sense of helpless vulnerability.

Daily conversion of heart can happen in such simple moments as the choice to greet someone uncongenial to us with kindness and genuine interest rather than avoidance or anger. It can happen in such terrible moments as the loss of a loved one, which of course requires a period of grieving, but eventually presents possibilities for building a new kind of life, or becoming active in a way to assure that others need not suffer as your loved one did. Conversion can happen even in an emotional breakdown, when the accumulated burden of secrets, lies, and enabling of others can no longer be borne; if the past is faced honestly (and at best, with support), genuine alternatives for new life can present themselves where before there was only darkness. Conversion can happen when we are presently stifled by fear and the overwhelming desire for security, but we choose to take even a small step in openness and vulnerability toward who or what we fear. During such times, it is well to have a friend, a guide, and/or a community to stand beside you. Karl Durkheim, believing that the way of transformation can be a painful one, encourages us to deal with hard times by seeking friends "who will faithfully and inexorably help us to risk ourselves, so that we may endure the suffering and pass courageously through it," able then to encounter new depths of the Ground of Being and the possibilities of new life.[6]

Our newspaper recently reported on a project of the New Story Leadership organization to bring together small groups of young adults from historically hostile countries for two weeks, simply to hear each other as people like themselves. This particular group included young people from Israel and Palestine. Several shared that their families did not want them to come, or that they had been criticized for their Facebook postings about cease-fires and the need for more reflection on both sides. One spoke of knowing children at home who were killed by the military actions of the "other side" who claimed the bombing was "self defense." All agreed there were uncomfortable moments—sometimes very uncomfortable, but they were willing to experiment with creating a "new story" for themselves and for their people. One expressed the overall spirit: "Life begins at the end of your comfort zone. I'm definitely not in my comfort zone. But I'm here."[7] These young people are risking ongoing daily conversion.

At the heart of ongoing daily conversion is a kind of vulnerability. When I encounter something that challenges my basic life orientation, I will undoubtedly feel emotionally assaulted or anxious. What do I do with those feelings? Perhaps my usual response is to defend my position, challenging the other. Possibly my response is to back away, desiring to ignore the challenge and ease my anxiety. In general, my first response is probably that I am "right," and whatever disturbs me is wrong. But what if I take a moment to consider that anxiety may actually be a spiritual call, a moment that changes me and drives me to conversion?[8] What if I respond to the challenge by asking myself how I might become a more whole person by taking the unwelcome change seriously as potentially bearing a genuine gift to me?

Robert Kegan describes what he calls a "fifth order of consciousness," in which we learn to greet disturbances in our ordinary reality as able to offer us a greater wholeness of being than we have heretofore known.[9] In the example given above of the young people meeting others of "the enemy," such a response might mean not that they abandon previous loyalties, but that they now see them in a broader context, in which, as human beings, *both sides* have similar rights and needs. In the case of an arguing couple, it might mean that rather than reaching only a mutually acceptable compromise, each partner adopts some of the other's perspective so that both become slightly different people, more well-rounded than either was before the argument.

It may be easier to imagine willingness to be so vulnerable and open to God than with other human beings or nations. But spiritual tradition suggests that we are in fact encountering God's call to us in each and every time we encounter a challenge to change. As Joan Chittister observes, the truth about life is that we *are* vulnerable from all sides, and "it takes a great deal of living to discover that, actually, vulnerability comes to us more as friend than as enemy," because vulnerability bonds us to one another and helps us become what we ourselves have the potential to be.[10] Vulnerability is the secret to the practice of resilience.

Conversion of heart or resilience refers to the daily dying to self, essential to ongoing growth in the spiritual life. American Benedictine Mary Forman expresses this as the discipline of "unknowing" what we think we know, so as to be embraced by the surprise of the Divine where we had not expected it.[11] When we insist on controlling things, on keeping matters in comfortable and familiar order, we limit the possible outcomes to what we can imagine. Conversion calls us to give up the quest for certainty and even coherence in our spiritual growth, acknowledging our own shadows, recognizing whatever distorts, handicaps, and arrests us. When we live the pain of necessary losses, we gradually learn to look at the world realistically, while yet trusting that the living God is indeed presiding over the apparent chaos in our lives and elsewhere, bringing forth a pattern yet invisible to us.

Chaos in the World

So far this chapter has concentrated on experiencing uncertainty and practicing resilience at a personal level, learning to accept disorientation and change as essential gifts in personal spiritual growth. We cannot stop here, however, since so much of our experience of the world today is of uncertainty and chaos on a much larger scale. James Huchington joins many commentators in observing that modern Western culture is in the midst of another "lurching shift in worldviews," and that the difficulties in living through one of these somewhat sudden shifts in orientation include not only anxiety and uncertainty but also hope and anticipation."[12] The question such shifts bring to the fore is, how do we go about living a spiritual life and maintaining hope in a world so full of complexity and change? I have been involved in many dinner conversations in recent years that end with everyone throwing up their hands in despair at our inability to understand or affect social trends. So a book on spiritual practice necessarily endeavors to address the anxiety and discouragement that so many of us feel about our world, not just about our personal spiritual lives. As we know, our spiritual lives do not end at the doors of our homes and churches, and as Gustavo Gutierrez points out, one of our primary responsibilities as Christians is to proclaim and shelter "the gift of the Kingdom of God in the heart of human history."[13] Other religious and spiritual groups speak of this same obligation in their own language. The public mixture of uncertainty and hope create the "soup" our spiritual practice must "stir" today.

Experiencing Chaos

Do any of us *like* change when it comes upon us without our consent? Perhaps some of us do, but it seems that most of us respond with anxiety and fear to disorientation in our lives. Such feelings are magnified when we are confused, having little understanding of where the change is coming from or what kind of future it will produce. The unknown brings with it a fear of loss, of things ending and falling apart. We've heard about entropy, the theory in physics that every isolated system eventually disintegrates into total disorder, and there's a suspicion that the unwanted changes of our times are signs of pending chaos. If you'll bear with me for a moment, I'd like to explain that I was considerably heartened a few years ago when I realized that more often than not, although chaos starts with confusion and complexity, it gradually resolves into new patterns. In other words, when an old order begins the process of radical change, the initial bewildering complexity gradually reveals new configurations of more flexible and adaptive forms.

Physicist and psychologist John Van Eenwyk has actually found similarities between healthy growth in the soul and the dynamics of chaos theory. He suggests that the world view we are leaving was interested primarily in analysis, prediction, explanation, and control (and, I would add, a relationship with God that was sturdy, predictable, and certain).[14] In contrast, it may be that in our time, order and stability may not be all that desirable for healthy physical systems nor for maturing souls. Perhaps we are living in an emergent time of chaos, and our work is the spiritual task of resilience, allowing new and more expansive and compassionate forms to emerge. The important role of chaos in creating space for needed new possibilities reminds me of the metaphor offered in the sequence of Jesus's death and resurrection. Death has not the last word, but in some important way is the doorway for new life.

An example emerges from a course I took as a young adult. One evening our teacher divided us into two groups, keeping aside three folks who were to judge a contest between the two groups. Each group was to build a tower with tinker toys in a specified time, and at the end the two towers would be assessed for stability, height, and beauty. Our group was told to function in an "orderly" way, hierarchically, with one team for the base and another for the tower. No worker was allowed to speak with another one except through the supervisors, sending any necessary message up and down the structure in both directions. We didn't know that the other group, in contrast, was completely unstructured! And to add to our dismay, the free-form group won on all three measures!

The lesson was that when tasks are not routine, hierarchy or fixed order impedes response. The apparent "chaos" of a bunch of people all doing the same thing at the same time worked better *for the creative task* than did the orderly stable pattern. A current saying reveals the same truth, that there is no point in continuing to try solving a problem with the same tools that have failed many times before.

In practical terms, what might chaos and resilience look like today? Technically, chaos is characterized primarily by complexity and variety. Complexity we understand all too well, as referring to a bewildering variety of possibilities. A cartoon reveals complexity in a few sketched lines—a spouse standing in front of the bread counter on his cell phone, asking "What kind of bread am I supposed to get?!" A loaf of bread used to be a loaf of bread; now we must choose between white and wheat (or rye, pumpernickel, and multigrain), regular or gluten free, sliced or whole loaf, hot dog or hamburger buns, and so forth. With various intermarriages, we no longer have terms for important family relationships (how am I related to my daughter's husband's children's families?). We even have so many denominations in Christianity, not to mention divisions among Buddhists, Hindus, Jews, and

Muslims, that we no longer know whether we are all even in the same religion, or if it even matters. It would be funny, if it were not so serious, for the incredible amount of complexity in the world today erodes a sense of stability in the certainties we used to take for granted, and that leaves us anxious and troubled, with little sense of how to get a handle even on the boundaries of our own lives. As we become aware of how painful complexity can be, can we also glimpse a possibility that our "boundaries" may have been too narrow, enclosing too small an area of concern? In the connective tissue of the global world today, possibly our self-righteous nationalism is a barrier to the new world breaking through.

The second major characteristic of chaos is variety or difference. Our world is increasingly awash in many loud voices, each claiming priority. All the talk about "politically correct" language, however tongue-in-cheek, does point toward the fact that voices previously muted or marginalized are no longer willing to let others speak for them. And I think that these additional voices add immeasurably to the richness of our communal conversation. However, at the moment, there is no common understanding of the ground in which conversation is held. And one highly distressing effect of that lack is the strong polarization in so many of our institutions. We may bring our legislatures to an absolute standstill soon, and that prospect is abhorrent to one committed to the process of democracy. However, even here I believe God offers a way through for us. Each of us can and must do all we can to bring the loving realm of God into being here and now without being wedded to what we believe is a desired outcome. It may indeed be that many of our major existing institutions are passing away in this historical space of chaos; if so, it is likely that the diminishment is occurring because of a failure to respect one another, and because of our failure to practice resilience.

I often turn to memories or stories of past events that seemed to be disasters at the time to remind myself that this is still God's world and God is always working to bring forth new life, however it may seem to us. One of my cherished stories is that of the vision Benedict had shortly before his death that his beloved monastery would soon be destroyed. I can't imagine how hard it must have been to receive and live with that insight, because he had worked for twenty-five years to build up a holy community. His vision was a true one, and after his death, a group of marauding gangsters attacked the monastery and destroyed all the buildings. However, not a single monk lost his life, and all fled to Rome into the arms and welcoming monastery of a young fellow named Gregory who would soon become Pope, and would write the only Life of St. Benedict we have. Not only that, but Gregory sent a missionary group to the northern isles (Britain) and they brought the gospel and Benedict's simple wisdom across Europe and to England. The destruction of the monastery was a disaster, yet the spread of the gospel to such further regions created an outcome Benedict could never have envisioned.

Recall that it is not only in Jesus's passion that the Bible offers a powerful metaphor for the emergence of new life, but also in its very first verses. Genesis 1:2 tells us of the central role of primordial chaos: "The earth was without form and void and darkness was upon the face of the deep and the Spirit of God was moving over the face of the waters." Without form or substance, chaos responds in unspoken anticipation to the liberating act of divine creation.[15] The God who is Mystery bears within the infinite potential of chaos to be dynamic, threatening and productive.

How can this look at the creative possibilities of uncertainty and chaos help us find ways to be hopeful in light of the chaotic state of our world? And how do we build a spiritual practice that honors the mysteries of compassion in such a world?

Seeing Clearly

The first step in this work is to look honestly, see clearly, and speak the truth about what we see. As Jesus asks us, "Can you not read the signs of the times?" (Matt. 16:3). Often our "reading" of present day signs is shaped by pre-judgments and wishful thinking. Sr. Ishpriya calls for "the steady gaze of perception sharpened and freed by the serious practice of contemplative prayer or meditation," which enables all events to speak the Mystery without overwhelming us.[16] She recalls a long conversation with a young Hindu monk covering the awesome and terrible matters which afflict our world today, and was struck by his likeness to Jesus in his simple recognition and calm realism. Can we see these events clearly without trying to minimize or exaggerate their importance, or distort their message into what is more agreeable to us? When we cannot see clearly what now exists, how can we discern the emerging form of the yet unseen?

Walter Brueggemann responds boldly to Ishpriya's challenge for clear thinking. First, he observes that many of us are weary—with anxiety fed by our denial of what is, and we are also heavy laden—with coercion about ways to work and ways to think that are fed by our despair; and both anxiety and coercion lose their power where truth and hope are told.[17] Then Brueggemann (admitting a slight overstatement) boldly describes our current "mode of social existence" in the following way. Dominant social culture:

- imagines a centered, secure, well-ordered world that permits absolutes and certitudes;
- imagines a normative security of *legitimacy and conformity* that enforces norms about life, finance, the military, and sexuality and imposes a high degree of conformity on all members of the community;
- is largely committed to *acquisitiveness and to the uncriticized centrality of the market,* not only in the economy but in all social relationships;
- is *committed to 24/7 about everything,* about work, about play and self-indulgence, about instant availability by cell phone or whatever, with no space left for the human spirit nor for the underneath mystery; and
- is a culture of *assertive initiative taking* without openness for mutuality or mood or practice of receptivity (even for yielding prayer).[18]

This list is disturbing. Perhaps some part of our minds acknowledges its truth, but if we take it seriously, it can create anxiety and fear. Yet if our previous assessment is true that the uncertainties characteristic of personal spiritual growth are both necessary and helpful, then we must also consider that the challenges and distortions in our communal and cultural lives have the potential to be redemptive, if we can learn to live well in response to them. Lists like Brueggemann's may help us to see more clearly that elements of Western culture may need to be contested by Christ-like people.

Pause to reflect: *His list itself is a challenge, but perhaps it might be useful to talk about Brueggemann's assessment with others in our various religious communities. How clearly does he see? Can we also see some of these dynamics? Do we agree that some of them have the effect of reducing the livability of our communities? Can we begin to make changes in our own lives that might remove some of these imbalances? And what spiritual tools might help us make adjustments to create more healthy communities?*

Although it may have seemed that there is a linear relationship in the metaphor of movement from stability to death to new life, it is more likely all these elements are present at any one time, and part of our seeing clearly may be also to observe and support the growth of new life where we find it.

A Spiritual Response of Resilience

As we review the spiritual practice recommended in the earlier personal section of this chapter, we observe a pattern of practice that can be helpful in the larger public arenas of our lives. The *first* element is a deep confidence in God's presence in history and in us, however events might seem to us. The *second* is learning to see unsought and unwelcome assaults on our previous reality as potential opportunities for greater wholeness in ourselves and in the world, instead of allowing ourselves to sink into despair. Whatever happens, whatever loss, whatever pain, we know that Christ is our companion in suffering. And the *third* is practicing the response of resilience—bending with new movements rather than holding rigidly to old ideas and behaviors in such a way that causes us to break under the stress.

Each of these elements of spiritual practice can be described as an exercise in vulnerability. Even the word may cause us to back off. Our culture seems to have a predisposition to the view that vulnerability is bad and self-sufficiency is good. But as Joan Chittister observed earlier in this chapter, spiritual maturity brings with it an increasing awareness that vulnerability is our friend, for it enables us to be open to the gifts continuously offered in our world. Vulnerability, as I am using the word, does not mean being a doormat, nor being foolish in opening ourselves to evil. But in a world where we are increasingly hiding behind our own psyches or our own closed doors (if we have them), there is room to consider something other than the opposite extreme.

I was always taught that strangers were dangerous, that even among primitive people, any newcomer was greeted warily, because they were probably "different." This is actually a very strange and ideological point of view. Why assume that those different from us have malicious intent? In the radical polarizations of our day, we are told that women should distrust men and vice versa. Conservatives should distrust liberals and vice versa. Persons with different skin colors or languages are ignored or marginalized. Think of what we lose in opportunities to grow and learn from those who see the world differently than we do. Many who travel the world in these days find much to admire and appreciate in quite different ways of thinking and behaving. And some contemporary thought raises "difference" to the status of a valued treasure.

But, making due allowances for reasonable risk, spiritual vulnerability is more than mere curiosity or tolerance. Theologian Dorothy Soelle writes of a "window of vulnerability," not as it is used by military strategists to identify a gap in the defense system, but rather as a window toward heaven, because it is a sign of relationship, receptivity, and communication.[19] She points out that in general our culture lives with a picture of the hero as the strongest and invulnerable warrior, to which she contrasts "the unarmed carpenter's son from Galilee."[20] I also have often puzzled how important it seems to be to us to refer to God as "almighty," when God was born among us as a vulnerable human infant, and died among us on the cross. To live in inward relationship with Christ would seem to require the practice of vulnerability.

Might it be possible that the practice of vulnerability—openness to the other—is a secret which gives us inner power and strength with which to bear life's challenges? Might it be that the most damning item on Brueggemann's list of cultural problems is actually the last one: that we are a culture of *assertive initiative taking* without openness for mutuality or mood or practice of receptivity (even for yielding prayer)? Openness for mutuality and receptivity are qualities essential in the relationship with God, otherwise we are holding off the reality of the Divine. Mystic Meister Eckhardt promises that "God longs for nothing from you more than that you should emerge from yourself in accord with your being as a creature, and that you should admit God within yourself."[21] The ability to surrender to God is surely related to our ability to be vulnerable to one another.

The example of vulnerability and resilience that jumps into my mind is that of my granddaughter and my niece, both of whom at very young ages went to "Mommy and Me" yoga classes. The two-year-olds could easily slip into what is called the "downward-facing dog" pose, in which arms and legs press down into the floor, while the buttocks are pressed high in the air, in an upside-down V shape. For me, this is an exceedingly strenuous pose, and I sweat mightily if required to hold it for long. But the little girls popped right up in exactly the correct way, giggling a bit with the fun of it all. Over time in my growth into "adulthood," I have unlearned vulnerability and lost resilience, and have to work hard to relearn it. But the little children knew it by heart.

Neither vulnerability nor resilience is easy. Both require regular practice in many daily opportunities; both require facing our fears of inadequacy, our anxiety about security, and our actual need for others. Yet as Moses assures God's people, these practices and gifts are not in the sky where we must fly to get them; they are not in the deeps where we must swim to get them; they are here, in our mouths and in our hearts, ready for us to accept them (Deut. 30:11-14). As we continue in our practice of these essential spiritual tools, gradually they bring us hope. Resilience teaches us that the Spirit is alive and vital in our world, reaching out always for our good.

SAMPLE EXERCISES

Befriending Disturbances and Doubts

Take time to reflect on your current pattern of response to disturbances and doubts in your life. Do you struggle to change things, or get upset when things do not turn out as you had planned, or are you someone who can easily adapt if things unfold in a way you did not imagine? Are you frequently disappointed in yourself or others, or do you enjoy being surprised by the diversity in life? Do you feel that uncertainty is a sign of diminished faith? Spend some time over the course of a week observing your reaction to how life flows internally for you. Practice befriending disturbances; actually seeing them as gifts that might lead you down a new path. Practice welcoming doubts as a way of learning to tolerate the reality of unknowing.

Speaking Truth to Chaos

All of us have aspects of our lives that are chaotic and which fill us with anxiety. In this practice you will choose one or two concerns from your own life on which to focus and then find a word of truth to speak to it in order to diminish its power. Center in prayer and allow one concern to arise. Allow it to come fully into focus. Then ask God to provide a word of truth for you to hold against the power of that sense of chaos. Some phrases that are true and grounding may be, "God is aware of this concern and has my best interest at heart." Or perhaps, "This problem is not bigger than God's love and care for me." Listen and let the Spirit offer you grace.

A New Way Challenge

Part of learning how to bend in resilience is also woven into learning new pathways and exploring other traditions. For this practice take some time to explore the other faith traditions in your community and choose to visit one of their worship services. Challenge yourself to be open to the movement of the Holy Spirit and resist evaluation and judgment. See if you can experience God in a totally different context than the one to which you are accustomed.

FOR FURTHER READING

Anonymous. *The Cloud of Unknowing.* Edited by William Johnston. Doubleday/ Image Books, 1973.

Walter Brueggemann. *Praying the Psalms.* Winona, MN: St. Mary's Press, 1973.

Pema Chodron. *Living Beautifully with Uncertainty and Change.* Boston: Shambhala Publications, 2012.

James E. Huchingson. *Pandemonium Tremendum: Chaos and Mystery in the Life of God.* Cleveland, OH: Pilgrim Press, 2001.

Robert Kegan, "Conflict, Leadership and Knowledge Creation," Joann Wolski Conn, *Women's Spirituality.* Mahweh, NJ: Paulist Press, 1996.

Diarmuid O'Murchu. *Quantum Theology: Spiritual Implications of the New Physics.* New York: Crossroad, 1998.

Dorothy Soelle. *The Window of Vulnerability.* Transl. Linda Maloney. Minneapolis, MN: Fortress Press, 1990.

Norvene Vest. *Re-Visioning Theology: A Mythic Approach to Religion.* Mahweh, NJ: Paulist Press, 2011.

Epilogue: The Goal of Practice

Humans, while certainly creatures and, as such, external to God,
are defined in their very nature *as being fully themselves*
only when in communion *with God.*
To become fully human, to realize our human potential,
we need to enter into communion with our Creator.
We can become ourselves only by transcending ourselves.

A.M. Allchin, quoting Athanasius

Theosis

In early Christian centuries, the Gospel was succinctly expressed as "God became human so that humans might become God." A.M. Allchin observes that this statement "necessarily implies that the Christian gospel cannot be simply fitted into the world as is now is. It involves radical transformation"—of our ideas about God, ourselves, and the world in which we live.[1] Perhaps we do not often consider that in some sense we are meant to become God, yet there is an utter truth in this statement. The meaning is not that as individuals we become God, but rather that as a community of Christians, each and all of us are invited to bear God in such a way as to transform our consciousness, shape our lives, and reveal God's glory in the world. The technical term for "becoming God" is *theosis*, or divinization. It may at first shock and dismay us to realize that we really are invited to take God into our lives until we ourselves are divinized, but that is the invitation.

Although the Gospel in the West has not always been preached to make this invitation clear, there is no doubt that the whole Christian tradition claims the full power of the Holy Spirit as available in and through us to "do greater things than these" (John 14:12). This is the goal of spiritual practice, to grow so intimately into union with God that not only we but the world are transformed.

We may prefer to use the language of Richard Hooker, who speaks eloquently of our *participation in God*. To begin with, Hooker sees the whole creation as drenched with Deity. It is not that God is confined in creation, but more like the way a great painting inevitably reveals its maker. For example, I can always recognize a van Gogh, a man not appreciated in his lifetime, yet one with an astonishingly rich and vibrant sense of the world. Van Gogh does not simply paint; he fills up the canvas with rich layers of vibrant color. Much as I have enjoyed copies of his work, I was stunned when I saw an original, so full of paint and color as to seem three dimensional, almost ready to jump off the wall into my arms. This is an image of the way God is present in nature, and if in nature, how much more in human beings, if we offer him ourselves.

It is in this sense that the Cappadocian Christians insist that God is present even in what we might think of as our "worst" qualities, our lust and anger. God does not stint in pouring the divine presence into our hearts; the only limits are those we set up to resist or distort it, or the ways we deflect it inappropriately. The desire, the longing, we sometimes experience for something more is God's way of communicating the Divine desire for union with us. We are creatures whose nature it is always to seek that which is beyond our nature, creatures made for self-transcendence. Such transcendence happens when we allow God full access to our hearts and minds and bodies, when we participate fully in being with God.

C. S. Lewis, known for his images of *sehnsucht*, longing, writes eloquently:

> We do not want merely to see beauty, though, God knows, even that is bounty enough. We want something else which we can hardly put into words—to be united with the beauty we see, to pass into it, to receive it into ourselves, to bathe in it, to become part of it. . . . At present we are on the wrong side of the door. We discern the freshness and purity of the morning, but they do not make us fresh and pure. . . . But the leaves of the New Testament are rustling with the rumor that it will not always be so.[2]

The goal of practice is to enter into union with God in such a way that it makes us fresh and pure, though of course, we may not know it consciously. Some of us may have the sense of being infused with the eyes and spirit of God, and many of us may not. It is enough that at heart we feel beauty and joy, and that we know we are of service in compassion with others.

Participation and Practice

If participation in God is fully the gift of God, why need we practice? No amount of practice will give us enough "points" to *deserve* union with God. Yet practice helps prepare us to receive the gift; with practice, we learn to know ourselves, to reduce our resistances, to become vulnerable. Without these preparations, it is unlikely that God will abide fully in us. Of course, with God anything is possible, and it is not for us either to judge others unworthy, or to envy what we think should already be ours.

The fundamental meaning of practice, as the term is used here, is that it combines the best of the old with the best of the new. Jesus charges those who are training for the kingdom of heaven to bring out of their treasure what is new and what is old (Matt. 13:52). I take this to mean honoring the best of what we have inherited, while also being open to the goodness of the new possibilities around us. We are to receive the gospel and find ways of sharing it that speak to people's hearts and minds today. Thus in this book, we have discussed many traditional practices, such as scripture, almsgiving and prayer (chapters 3, 4, and 5), restored the rightful place of gratitude and wonder/ imagination (chapters 2 and 6), emphasized the importance of integrity and social justice (chapters 7 and 8), and addressed the issue of sustaining faith and hope in the midst of change (chapter 9).

We do not expect that anyone will undertake all these practices at once. We are, after all, talking about a lifetime of spiritual growth. To me, one of the great joys of life with God is the realization that God fills our hearts in such a way that there is always more room to grow, or as St. Benedict says, God enlarges our hearts, strengthens our capacity to bear the darts of heavenly regard and support.

So take things one at a time; begin with a practice that particularly appeals to you as being important for you now, and work with that practice until it begins to seem habitual, at which point you may be ready to move on to another practice. Moving on does not mean setting aside the current practice, but rather allowing it to become so familiar that it no longer needs so much of your attention, having become a natural part of your daily rhythm.

You may wish to work through this whole book initially, alone or better with a group of people similarly inclined, and later return specifically to one or two of the practices which call to you now. Let the Spirit be your guide.

Participation in God and the World

Participation in God implies also participation in the world. Raymond Panikkar compares two overall approaches to the world: the way of simplicity and that of complexity. Panikkar honors a traditional path of simplicity, but also welcomes an emergent path of complexity. The traditional path seeks fullness of life through simplification while the emergent way tends to seek it through integration.[3] The first risks reductionism: the move toward simplification possibly rejects too much of the world and does violence to the real. The traditional spiritual path may be tempted to pessimism, finding the world too distracting or sinful. On the other hand, the emergent path risks gathering everything "found" without regard to its inherent value, in the move to find the goodness in complexity. The contemporary path is tempted to optimism, possibly ignoring or minimizing evil and suffering. In setting side by side these two spiritual paths, Panikkar acknowledges a conflict of interpretations and seeks to honor both sides, while trying to move toward a vision beyond either.

Central to the distinction between traditional and emergent paths is the move away from renunciation toward a hope for the *transformation* of all things. Emphasis is not so much on sin and suffering as rather on the harmonious embrace of everything, which is a bold shift, emphasizing inclusion rather than denial in the endeavor to midwife the world into the fullness implicit in its potential as God's self-giving.

The very word complexity suggests the connection of many ingredients so that they may fit together in a whole. Harmonious complexity assumes that there is no inherent incompatibility between and among the internal tendencies of the different elements to be joined and assumes it is possible to reconcile all the elements in a situation. But since things are not already joined and fitted together, harmonious complexity is not automatic; it means that *everything has to be transformed* in order that all may fit together. Such transformation is only authentic if it expresses a movement by which things become what they really are, toward the natural fullness of their being. And it requires the work of the Holy Spirit as well as the receptivity of the world.

If this path toward transformation is optimistic in its minimization of evil and its belief in the compatibility of all that is, it also reflects a kind of intentional and participatory presence that we have called the goal of practice. It does not emerge from a first naiveté of innocent hopefulness, but rather follows a journey of practice bringing self-awareness, a clear assessment of diversity and who benefits from existing ways, and awareness that change is likely to be challenged, coupled with a readiness to stand firm in the face of such challenge. Such engagement can only be undertaken with confidence that God is even now working through human lives to bring about transformation through what might sometimes appear to be failure or death. Although the emergent spiritual path to transformed life may bring suffering, it also brings discovery and is the means by which a new future may unfold.

Practice helps us glimpse and even begin to live into the joy which God has in the creation and creation's response to God. When we become conscious of this truth, we find ourselves awestruck in an experience of God's dynamic joy which changes all things. We find a new way of looking at things, a realization that we are able to respond to the world's problems, when we see that in the power of the gospel, the problems themselves are being changed, even as we ourselves are in the process of changing.[4] We find ourselves neither surrendering to nor escaping the world, but return to that wonderful source of energy in which the world is created and made for joy.

In the writing of this book, we found our minds drawn into a deep humility—both about the honor of being called to this work, and about how much we have yet to learn and live. At the same time, our hearts have begun to soar with the joy and possibility inherent in life with God. We hope these qualities will also be gifts to you as you read, ponder, and work with the practices offered in these pages. May God continue richly to bless you.

FOR FURTHER READING

A. M. Allchin. *Participation in God.* Wilton, CT: Morehouse-Barlow, 1988.
Annie Lamott. *Help, Thanks, Wow.* New York: Riverhead/Penguin, 2013.
Raimundo Panikkar. *Blessed Simplicity: The Monk as Universal Archetype.* New York: Seabury, 1982.

Richard Rohr. *A Lever and a Place to Stand: The Contemplative Stance, the Active Prayer.* Mahwah, NJ: Paulist Press, 2012.

Jean Vanier. *Becoming Human.* Mahwah, NJ: Paulist Press, 1998.

Norvene Vest. *Desiring Life.* Cambridge, MA: Cowley Publications, 2000.

James D. Whitehead and Evelyn Eaton Whitehead. *Nourishing the Spirit: The Healing Emotions of Wonder, Joy, Compassion, and Hope.* Maryknoll, NY: Orbis Books, 2012.

Notes

Chapter 1

1. The Venerable Bede, *A History of the English Church and People*, trans. Leo Sherley-Price (Baltimore: Penguin Classics, 1960), 124-25.
2. Evelyn Underhill, *Mysticism: A Study in Nature and Development of Spiritual Consciousness* (Maryknoll, NY: Orbis Books, 2003), 19.
3. Ibid., 25.
4. Huston Smith, *The Religions of Man* (New York: Harper & Row, 1958), adapted here from his pages, 32-46.
5. See for example John 1:39, Luke 10; 1-9, and Matt 9:9-14.
6. Ada Maria Isasi-Diaz, *Mujerista Theology: A Theology for the Twenty-First Century* (Maryknoll, NY: Orbis Books, 1996), 65, 125.
7. Josef Pieper, *About Love*, trans. Richard and Clara Winston (Chicago: Franciscan Herald Press, 1974), 25.
8. Robert Wuthnow. *After Heaven: Spirituality in American since the 1950s* (Berkeley: University of California Press, 1998).
9. Ibid., 7-8.
10. Ibid., 14.
11. Ibid., 16, italics mine.
12. Guigo II the Carthusian, *The Ladder of Monks*, trans. E. Colledge (Kalamazoo, MI: Cistercian Publications), 74.
13. John Chapman, *Spiritual Letters* (New York: Continuum/Burns & Oates, 2003), 155.

Chapter 2

1. Robert Browning, *Pippa Passes*, originally published in 1841 as the first volume of his *Bells and Pomegranates* series.
2. Tilden Edwards, *Living Simply through the Day* (Mahwah, NJ: Paulist Press, 1977).
3. Chenda Ngak, CBS NEWS, September 13, 2013, 9:59 a.m.
4. Thomas Keating, *Open Mind, Open Heart* (New York: Continuum Publishing, 1995), 20.
5. Robert Russell, *To Catch an Angel: Adventures in a World I Cannot See* (New York: Vanguard, 1962), 313.
6. Keating, *Open Mind, Open Heart*, 34.

Chapter 3

1. Urban T. Holmes III, *Ministry and Imagination* (New York: Seabury, 1981), 178-79.
2. Emily Dickenson, *Final Harvest*, selection by T. H. Johnson (Boston: Little, Brown, 1961) 248. "Tell all the truth but tell it slant—success in circuit lies. Too bright for our infirm delight the truth's superb surprise."
3. Education for Ministry Program, *Manual for Mentors* (Sewanee, TN: University of the South, School of Theology Programs Center, 1988), 28-29.
4. John Shea, *Stories of God: An Unauthorized Biography* (Chicago: Thomas More Press, 1978), 8.
5. Richard Kearney, *On Stories* (New York: Routledge, 2002), 125. His insights are also included in the following paragraphs.
6. I am indebted for these distinctions and insights to Urban T. Holmes III, *Ministry and Imagination* (New York: Seabury Press, 1981), especially chapter 7.
7. The Episcopal Church, *The Book of Common Prayer* (New York: Church Publishing, 1979), 372.
8. Holmes, ibid., 166.
9. Aristotle, *Poetics*, Introduction and Translation by Francis Fergusson (New York: Macmillan & Co., 1961), part VIII, 75.
10. Holmes, ibid., 167.
11. William Franke, *Dante's Interpretive Journey* (Chicago: University of Chicago Press, 1996), 20-1.
12. Michael Casey, *Sacred Reading: The Ancient Art of Lectio Divina* (Ligouri, MO: Liguori/Triumph Press, 52-53.
13. Susan Annette Muto, *A Practical Guide to Spiritual Reading* (Petersham, MA: St. Bede's Publications, 1994), 10 and the following section.
14. For further detail, see Casey, ibid., 54-57; and Norvene Vest, *No Moment Too Small* (Boston: Cowley, 1994), 68.
15. John Cassian, *Nicene and Post-Nicene Fathers of the Christian Church, Vol. XI*: Conference XIV:8, *Abbot Nesteros on Spiritual Knowledge*, trans. Matthew J. O'Connell (Collegeville, MN: Liturgical Press, 1979), 438.

Chapter 4

1. Marva J. Dawn, *Keeping the Sabbath Wholly: Ceasing, Resting, Embracing, Feasting* (Grand Rapids MI: Eerdmans Publishing Co., 1989).
2. Isaac Watts, *An arrangement of the Psalms, hymns, and spiritual songs of the Rev. Isaac Watts* (Lincoln & Edmands, 1821), 167.
3. New York Times, "Benefits of the Dinner Table Ritual," Laurie Tarkan, May 3, 2005.
4. Richard J. Foster, *Freedom of Simplicity* (HarperCollins, 2005), 66.

Chapter 5

1. Adapted from a booklet called *Simple Prayer* by Herrymon Maurer, published by Fellowship in Prayer in 1983.

2. Esther de Waal, *Seeking God* (Collegeville, MN: Liturgical Press, 1984), 153.

3. See chapter 3 for more information on *lectio divina*.

4. Catherine Keller, Lecture *Postmodernism, Culture and Religion* conference (Syracuse: Syracuse University, April 2007), italics mine.

5. Cynthia Bourgeault, *The Wisdom Way of Knowing* (San Francisco: Jossey-Bass, 2003), 31.

6. Ibid., 34.

7. Augustine of Hippo, "Commentary on I John," *Tractates* 4: PL 35, 2008-9.

8. See Anne Lamott's provocative title and book, *Help, Thanks, Wow* (New York: Penguin Books, 2013).

9. Adapted from a booklet called *A Power House of Prayer* (Winter Park, FL: Anglican Fellowship of Prayer, n.d.). The image of a "nosegay" after prayer comes from Francis de Sales, *The Introduction to a Devout Life* (New York: Image, 1972).

10. C. S. Lewis, *Letters to Malcolm: Chiefly on Prayer* (New York: Houghton Mifflin Harcourt, 1963).

11. "Peace Pilgrim," in *Fellowship of Prayer*, 36:6 (December, 1985). The Peace Pilgrim was a woman who committed herself to walk (within the United States) until there was world peace. Though it did not happen in her lifetime, she became a deeply prayerful woman.

12. *Book of Common Prayer* (New York: Seabury Press, 1979), 359 and 383 ff.

13. BCP, 268.

14. Known variously as a four-fold Franciscan/Benedictine blessing, it is easily found on the internet.

15. Here in chapter 1, page 11 and note 12, quoted from Guigo II the Catrthusian, *the Ladder of Monks*.

16. Bernard of Clairvaux, "Four Degrees of Love," quoted in *Devotional Classics*, Richard Foster and James Bryan Smith (New York: HarperOne, 1993), 41-44.

17. Anonymous, *Way of a Pilgrim*, and *Philokalia*, eds., Sts. Nicodemus and Macarius, trans. Palmer, Sherrard, & Ware (London: Faber and Faber, 1979).

18. John Cassian, *Conferences*, "Conference Ten On Prayer," trans. Colm Luibheid (Mahwah, NJ: Paulist Press, 1985)

19. Lauren Artress, *Walking a Sacred Path* (New York: Berkeley Publishing Group, 1995).

20. Benedict of Nursia, *The Rule*, trans. Timothy Fry, OSB, et al. (Collegeville, MN: Liturgical Press), chapter 16, p. 211.

21. For more information on this idea, consult Norvene Vest, *No Moment Too Small* (Boston: Cowley, 1994), 107ff.

22. Abraham Joshua Heschel, *The Sabbath* (New York: Farrar Strauss, 1951).

23. Thomas Keating, *Open Mind, Open Heart* (New York: Continuum, 2006).

Chapter 6

1. *Saint Teresa of Avila*, trans. Mirabai Starr (New York, Riverhead Books, 2003), 1.

2. Kelsey (Mahwah, NJ: Paulist Press, 1981), 64.
3. Gerald May, *Will and Spirit* (New York: Harper Collins, 1982), 53.
4. Walter Wink, *Transforming Bible Study* (Nashville: Abingdon Press, 1980), 24-25.
5. Stuart Brown with Christopher Vaughan, *Play: How It Shapes the Brain, Opens the Imagination, and Invigorates the Soul* (New York: Penguin, 2009), 40.
6. Suzanne Fincher, *Coloring Mandalas for Insight, Healing, and Self Expression* (Boston: Shambhala, 2000).

Chapter 7

1. C. S. Lewis, *Mere Christianity* (New York: Macmillan, 1952), 86.
2. Augustine of Hippo, *Commentary on the Lord's Sermon on the Mount*, trans. Denis J. Kavanagh, OSA (New York: Fathers of the Church, Inc., 1951).
3. Evagrius Pontus, *On Practice* and *Chapters on Prayer* (Collegeville, MN: Cistercian Publ., 1978) and John Cassian, *Conferences*, Trans. Colum Luibheid (Mahwah, NJ: Paulist, 1985) and *Institutes* (in *Nicene and Anti-Nicene Fathers*, trans. Edgar C. S. Gibson (Grand Rapids MI: Eerdmans, 1989).
4. Mary Margaret Funk, *Thoughts Matter: The Practice of the Spiritual Life* (New York: Continuum, 1998), 28. I am also indebted to her for many of the ideas in this section.
5. Some persons have bodies better attuned to "grazing" throughout the day, but they still maintain a moderate and appropriate body size. Grazing is also okay, as long as a natural rhythm and moderation are established and maintained.
6. Funk, ibid., 56.
7. Ibid., 57.
8. Luke Dysinger, OSB, lectures at St. Andrew's Abbey, Valyermo, California, during the 1990s, about Gregory of Nazianzan, Gregory of Nyssa, and Basil of Caesarea.
9. Funk, ibid., 66.
10. Rowan Williams, *Resurrection* (London: Darton, Longman, Todd, 2014).
11. F. M. Cornford, *Plato's Cosmology, on the Timaeus* (New York: Kegan Paul, 1937).

Chapter 8

1. Gerald May, *Will and Spirit* (New York: Harper Collins, 1982), 53.
2. https://www.stephenministries.org
3. Steve Corbett and Brian Fikkert, *When Helping Hurts: How to Alleviate Poverty Without Hurting the Poor . . . And Yourself* (Chicago: Moody Publishers, 2009), 78.

4. According to Lucinda Vardey, in *Mother Teresa: A Simple Path* (New York: Ballantine Books, 1995), 185, there was "a sign on the wall of Shishe Bhavan, the children's home in Calcutta." These eight verses are slightly modified from the "Paradoxical Commandments" attributed to Kent M. Keith in *The Silent Revolution: Dynamic Leadership in the Student Council* (Boston: Harvard Student Agencies, 1968).

Chapter 9

1. Obedience is a subject for another place. Resources include my own *Friend of the Soul*, and many other books, notably Esther de Waal's *Seeking God* (Collegeville, MN: Liturgical Press, 1984).
2. For more on the important role of spiritual imagination, see my *Re-Visioning Theology*, part one (New York: Paulist, 2011).
3. C. S. Lewis, *A Grief Observed* (New York: Seabury Press, 1961), 51.
4. Walter Brueggemann, *Praying the Psalms* (Winona, MN: St. Mary's Press, 1973), and *Mandate to Difference* (Louisville KY: Westminster John Knox, 2007) 44.
5. Carolyn Gratton, *The Art of Spiritual Guidance* (New York: Crossroad, 1992), 40.
6. Karlfried Gras von Durkheim, *The Way of Transformation* (n.p.; n.d.).
7. Karen Chen reporting for the *Washington Post*, July 30, 2014.
8. Soren Kierkegaard, quoted in Dorothy Soelle, *The Window of Vulnerability* (Minneapolis: Fortress Press, 1990), 118.
9. Robert Kegan, "Conflict, Leadership, and Knowledge Creation," in Joann Wolski Conn's *Women's Spirituality* (Mahwah, NJ: Paulist Press, 1996), 146.
10. Joan D. Chittister, *Heart of Flesh* (Grand Rapids, MI: Eerdmans, 1998).
11. Mary Forman, OSB, "Reflections on Encounters of a Mystery-ous Kind," *American Monastic Newsletter* 23:2 (1998), 2.
12. James Huchington, 37-38.
13. Gustavo Gutierrez, *A Theology of Liberation: History, Politics, and Salvation*, trans. St. Caridad Inda and John Eagleson (Maryknoll, NY: Orbis Books, 1973), 11.
14. John van Eenwyk, *Archetypes and Strange Attractors* (Toronto: Inner City Books, 1997).
15. Huchington, ibid., 100.
16. Sr. Ishpriya, "No More Sea," *The Way* (UK), October, 1995.
17. Brueggemann, *Mandate to Difference*, ibid., 45.
18. Brueggemann himself takes the next step, recommending a few key spiritual practices to minimize the discouraging effects of these cultural norms.
    • Consider choosing to be somewhat marginal, even "exiled," from the mainstream, in order to see more clearly;
    • Others belong with us and for us and are welcome as we are welcomed (including "red" or "blue" neighbors);
    • Generosity to the neighbor creates new possible futures;
    • Sabbath rest redeems our lives from the frantic rat-race; and
    • Yielding and relinquishing in prayer is a proper human mode given the Holy One who loves us. Ibid., 64.

19. Dorothy Soelle offers the idea of vulnerability as open practice in *The Window of Vulnerability*, transl. Linda Maloney (Minneapolis: Fortress Press, 1990), ix-x.

20. Ibid. xi.

21. Meister Eckhart, in Matthew Fox, *Breakthrough: Meister Eckhart's Creation Spirituality in New Translation* (Garden City, NY: Doubleday, 1980), sermon 6.

Epilogue

1. A. M. Allchin, *Participation in God* (Wilton, CN: Morehouse/Barlow, 1988), 1.

2. C. S Lewis, *Transpositions and Other Essays* (Oxford, UK: Oxford University Press, 1946), 31.

3. Raimundo Panikkar, *Blessed Simplicity: The Monk as Universal Archetype* (New York: Seabury, 1982), 11.

4. Allchin, ibid., 4.

CPSIA information can be obtained
at www.ICGtesting.com
Printed in the USA
LVHW110520060819
626642LV00001B/6/P